DEEP LEARNING

S. Nithya
Associate Professor,
Dept of CSE, Sathyabama Institute
of Science and Technology

Nancy Noella R. S.
Associate Professor,
Dept of CSE, Sathyabama Institute
of Science and Technology

V. Gowri Manohari
Associate Professor,
Dept of CSE, Sathyabama Institute
of Science and Technology

KHANNA BOOK PUBLISHING CO. (P) Ltd.
4C/4344, Ansari Road, Darya Ganj,
New Delhi, India

Sathyabama Institute of Science and Technology
Jeppiaar Nagar, Rajiv Gandhi Salai,
Chennai, Tamilnadu, India

Dear Readers,

To prevent the piracy, this book is secured with HIGH SECURITY HOLOGRAM on the front title cover. In case you don't find the hologram on the front cover title, please write us to at contact@khannabooks.com or whatsapp us at +91-99109 09320 and avail special gift voucher for yourself.

Specimen of Hologram on front Cover title:

Moreover, there is a SPECIAL DISCOUNT COUPON for you with EVERY HOLOGRAM.

How to avail this SPECIAL DISCOUNT:

Step 1: Scratch the hologram
Step 2: Under the scratch area, your "coupon code" is available
Step 3: Logon to www.khannabooks.com
Step 4: Use your "coupon code" in the shopping cart and get your copy at a special discount
Step 5: Enjoy your reading!

Thanks,
Khanna Publishing House

ISBN: 978-93-55388-19-3

DEEP LEARNING
by **S. Nithya; Nancy Noella R. S.; V. Gowri Manohari**

First Edition: 2026

To view complete list of books, please scan the QR Code:

Published by:
Khanna Book Publishing Co. (P) Ltd.
CIN: U22110DL1998PTC095547

Visit us at: www.khannabooks.com
Write us at: contact@khannabooks.com

Printed in Bharat.

Preface

Deep learning has revolutionized the field of Artificial Intelligence, significantly advancing the capabilities of computers in areas such as image recognition, natural language processing, robotics, and healthcare. As a subfield of Machine Learning, Deep Learning utilizes Artificial Neural Networks with multiple layers to extract and learn patterns from vast amounts of data. This book covers Sathyabama University Syllabus and is designed to provide students with a structured and comprehensive introduction to Deep Learning, equipping them with both theoretical knowledge and practical applications.

The primary objective of this book is to bridge the gap between fundamental concepts and real-world applications of Deep Learning. It covers essential topics, including neural networks, backpropagation, optimization techniques, convolutional neural networks, recurrent neural networks, generative models, and the latest advancements such as transformers and self-supervised learning. Each chapter is designed to progressively build the reader's understanding, reinforced with hands-on exercises, code implementations, and case studies.

By the end of this book, students will not only grasp the theoretical underpinnings of deep learning but also gain practical experience through real-world implementations. We hope that this book serves as a valuable resource for students, researchers, and practitioners who seek to deepen their knowledge and contribute to the ever-growing field of deep learning.

We extend our gratitude to all the researchers and educators whose contributions have shaped this field, and we invite readers to explore, experiment, and innovate as they embark on their deep learning journey.

Author(s)

Nithya S

Nancy Noella R S

Gowri Manohari V

Contents

UNIT 1

Introduction to Machine Learning (ML)

1.1 INTRODUCTION

Machine learning is a data analysis technique that automates the creation of analytical models. As a branch of artificial intelligence, it enables systems to learn from data, recognize patterns, and make decisions with minimal human involvement.

Example: Image recognition, Speech recognition, Medical diagnosis, Statistical arbitrage, Predictive analytics, etc.

1.1.1 Artificial Intelligence, Machine Learning and Deep Learning

Artificial Intelligence (AI) refers to a program that demonstrates cognitive abilities similar to those of humans. One of its core principles is enabling computers to think like humans and solve problems in a similar manner.

Any computer program that exhibits traits such as self-improvement, learning through inference, or performing basic human-like tasks—such as image recognition and language processing—is considered a form of AI.

The field of AI encompasses subfields like machine learning and deep learning.

Machine learning (ML) is an AI approach that enables computers to optimize performance criteria using example data or past experiences.

Deep Learning (DL) is a more advanced subset of machine learning that employs complex methods to tackle more challenging problems.

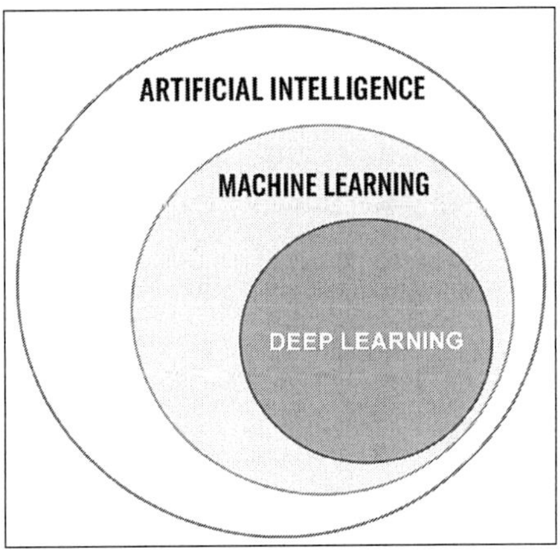

Figure 1.1: *Artificial Intelligence, Machine Learning and Deep Learning*

1.1.2 Types of Machine Learning Algorithms

These are three types of machine learning:

1. Supervised Learning
2. Unsupervised Learning
3. Reinforcement Learning

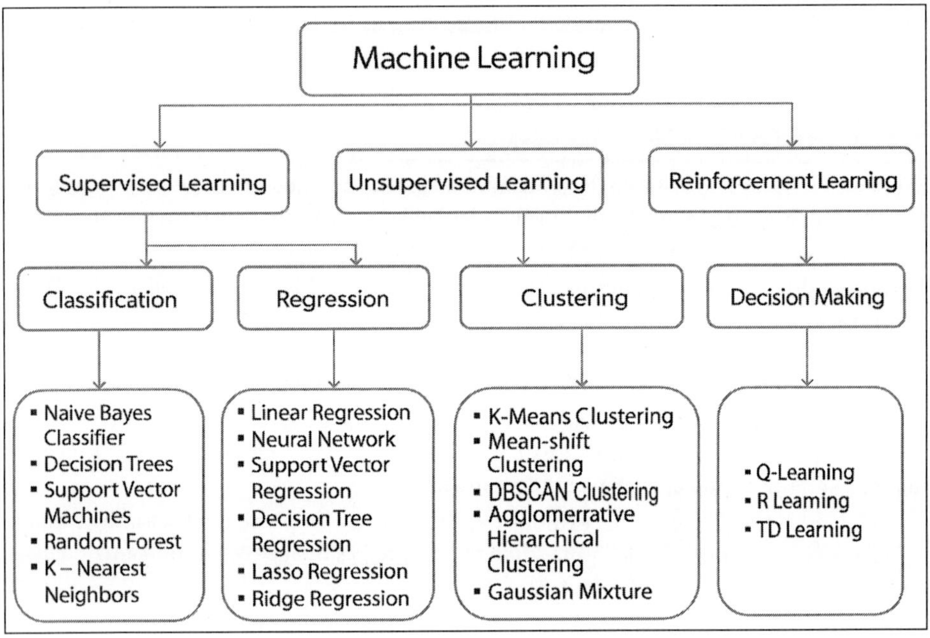

***Figure 1.2:** Classification of Machine Learning*

1. Supervised Learning

- Supervised learning is one of the fundamental types of machine learning.
- In this approach, the algorithm is trained using **labelled data.**
- A small training dataset, which is a subset of a larger dataset, is provided to the algorithm. This dataset helps the algorithm understand the nature of the problem, the possible solutions, and the key data points involved.
- Once the training is complete, the algorithm gains insight into the data structure and the connection between input and output variables.
- The trained model is then applied to the final dataset, where it continues to learn in a similar manner as it did with the training data.
- Examples include risk assessment, image classification, fraud detection, and spam filtering.

How Supervised Learning Works?

In supervised learning, models are trained using labelled dataset, where the model learns about each type of data. Once the training process is completed, the model is tested on the basis of test data (a subset of the training set), and then it predicts the output.

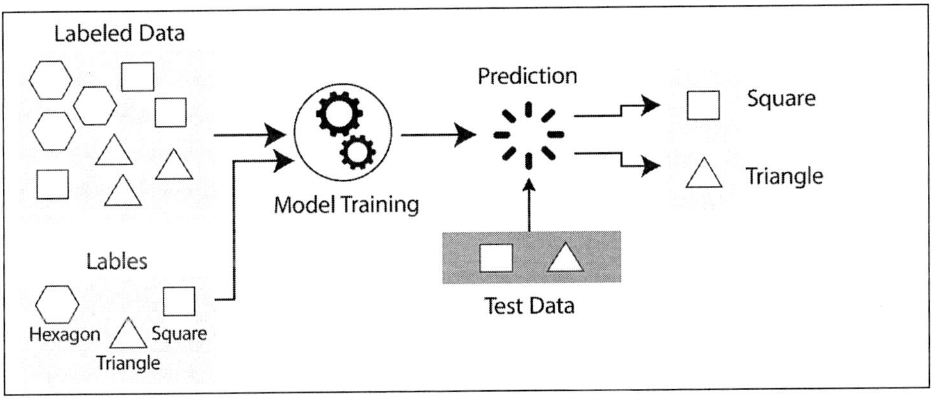

Figure 1.3: *Supervised Learning*

Suppose we have a dataset of different types of shapes which includes square, rectangle, triangle, and Polygon. Now the first step is that we need to train the model for each shape.

- If the given shape has four sides, and all the sides are equal, then it will be labelled as a Square.
- If the given shape has three sides, then it will be labelled as a triangle.
- If the given shape has six equal sides, then it will be labelled as hexagon.
- Now, after training, we test our model using the test set, and the task of the model is to identify the shape. The machine is already trained on all types of shapes, and when it finds a new shape, it classifies the shape on the bases of a number of sides, and predicts the output.

Advantages of Supervised Learning

- With the help of supervised learning, the model can predict the output on the basis of prior experiences.
- In supervised learning, we can have an exact idea about the classes of objects.

Disadvantages of Supervised Learning

- Supervised learning models are not suitable for handling complex tasks.
- Supervised learning cannot predict the correct output if the test data is different from the training dataset.
- Training required lots of computation times.

2. Unsupervised Learning

- Unsupervised machine learning has the advantage of processing **unlabelled data**, eliminating the need for human intervention to make datasets machine-readable. This enables the algorithm to handle significantly larger datasets efficiently.
- In supervised learning, labels help the algorithm determine precise relationships between data points. However, in unsupervised learning, the absence of labels leads to the formation of hidden structures within the data.
- The algorithm identifies relationships in an abstract way without human input, allowing it to uncover patterns autonomously.

- In supervised learning, labels help the algorithm determine precise relationships between data points. However, in unsupervised learning, the absence of labels leads to the formation of hidden structures within the data. The algorithm identifies relationships in an abstract way without human input, allowing it to uncover patterns autonomously.
- These hidden structures contribute to the flexibility of unsupervised learning algorithms. Unlike supervised learning, which follows a predefined problem statement, unsupervised algorithms dynamically adjust to the data, modifying hidden structures as needed.
- This adaptability allows for greater post-deployment improvements compared to supervised learning algorithms.
- Examples: Principal Component Analysis (PCA) and clustering.

How Unsupervised Learning Works?

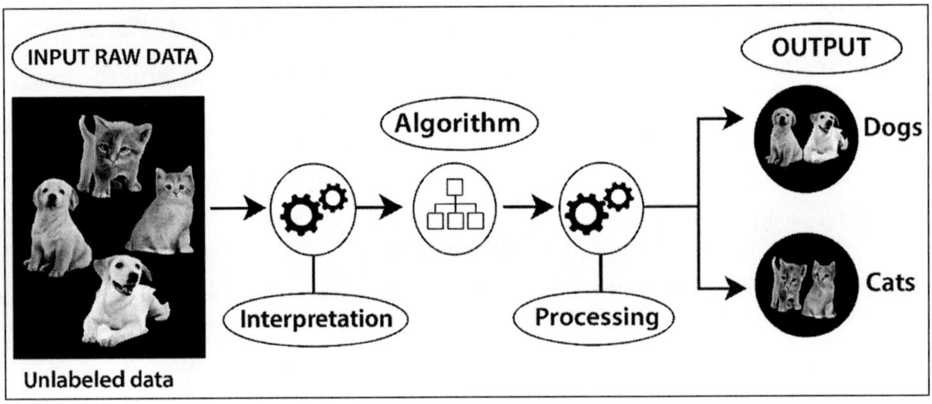

Figure 1.4: *Unsupervised Learning*

In this case, we use unlabeled input data, meaning it is not categorized, and corresponding outputs are not provided. This raw data is then fed into a machine learning model for training. The model first analyzes the data to identify hidden patterns and then applies appropriate algorithms, such as k-means clustering or decision trees. Once the algorithm is applied, it categorizes data objects into groups based on their similarities and differences.

Advantages of Unsupervised Learning

- Unsupervised learning is used for more complex tasks as compared to supervised learning because, in unsupervised learning, we don't have labelled input data.
- Unsupervised learning is preferable as it is easy to get unlabelled data in comparison to labelled data.

Disadvantages of Unsupervised Learning

- Unsupervised learning is intrinsically more difficult than supervised learning as it does not have corresponding output.
- The result of the unsupervised learning algorithm might be less accurate as input data is not labelled, and algorithms do not know the exact output in advance.

3. Semi-Supervised Learning

- It is a type of Machine Learning algorithm that represents the intermediate ground between Supervised and Unsupervised learning algorithms. It uses the combination of labeled and unlabeled data sets during the training period.
- The basic disadvantage of supervised learning is that it requires hand- labeling by ML specialists or data scientists, and it also requires a high cost to process. Further unsupervised learning also has a limited spectrum for its applications. To overcome these drawbacks of supervised learning and unsupervised learning algorithms, the concept of Semi-supervised learning is introduced.

Applications

- Speech Analysis
- Protein sequence classification
- Text document classifier

4. Reinforcement Learning (RL)

- Reinforcement Learning directly takes inspiration from how human beings learn from data in their lives. It features an algorithm that improves upon itself and learns from new situations using a trial-and- error method. Favourable outputs are encouraged or 'reinforced', and non-favourable outputs are discouraged or 'punished'.
- In every iteration of the algorithm, the output result is given to the interpreter, which decides whether the outcome is favourable or not.
- In case of the program finding the correct solution, the interpreter reinforces the solution by providing a reward to the algorithm. If the outcome is not favourable, the algorithm is forced to reiterate until it finds a better result. In most cases, the reward system is directly tied to the effectiveness of the result.
- In typical reinforcement learning use-cases, such as finding the shortest route between two points on a map, the solution is not an absolute value. Instead, it takes on a score of effectiveness, expressed in a percentage value. The higher this percentage value is, the more reward is given to the algorithm.
- Thus, the program is trained to give the best possible solution for the best possible reward.

Types of Reinforcement Learning

There are mainly two types of reinforcement learning, which are:

- **Positive Reinforcement:** Positive reinforcement in learning involves adding a stimulus to enhance the likelihood of the desired behavior recurring. It has a beneficial impact on the agent's behavior, strengthening its response. This type of reinforcement can lead to long-term behavioral changes. However, excessive positive reinforcement may result in an overload of states, potentially diminishing its effectiveness.
- **Negative Reinforcement:** Negative reinforcement is the opposite of positive reinforcement, as it strengthens the likelihood of a specific behavior recurring by removing or avoiding an unfavorable condition. Depending on the context

and behavior, it can sometimes be more effective than positive reinforcement. However, it only reinforces behavior to meet the minimum required standard.

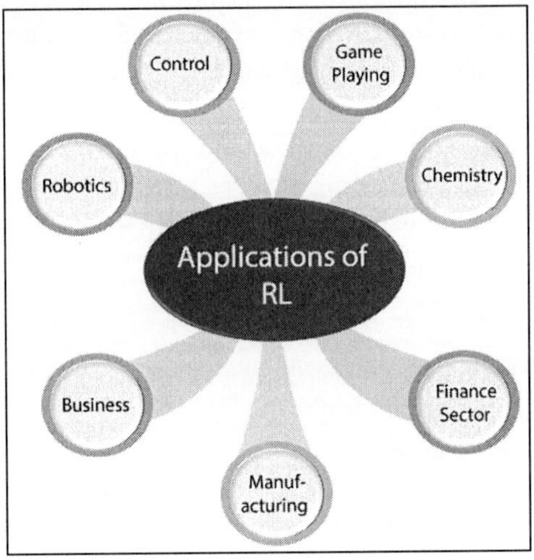

Figure 1.5: *Reinforcement Learning Applications*

Difference Between Supervised, Unsupervised and Reinforcement Learning

Criteria	Supervised ML	Unsupervised ML	Reinforcement ML
Definition	Learns by using labelled data	Trained using unlabelled data without any guidance.	Works on interacting with the environment
Type of data	Labelled data	Unlabelled data	No-predefined data
Type of problems	Regression and classification	Association and Clustering	Exploitation or Exploration
Supervision	Extra supervision	No Supervision	No Supervision
Algorithms	Linear Regression, Logistic Regression, VM, KNN, Etc.	K-Means, C-Means, Apriori	Q-Learning SARSA
Aim	Calculate outcomes	Discover underlying patterns	Learn a series of action
Application	Risk Evaluation, Forecast Sales	Recommendation System, Anomaly Detection	Self Driving Cars, Gaming, Healthcare

1.2 LINEAR MODELS

Linear models generate a formula to create a best-fit line to predict unknown values. Linear models are considered "old school" and often not as predictive as newer algorithm classes, but they can be trained relatively quickly and are generally more straightforward to interpret. A Simple linear model would be linear regression, and consider an example of using age to predict how much is spent in a week.

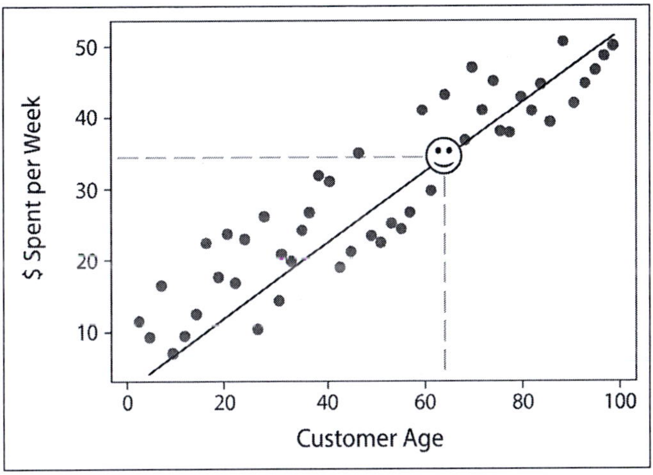

Figure 1.6: *Linear Models*

1.2.1 Support Vector Machine (SVM)

Support Vector Machine (SVM) is a widely used supervised learning algorithm, applicable to both classification and regression problems. However, it is most commonly used for classification tasks in machine learning. The objective of the SVM algorithm is to find the optimal line or decision boundary that divides an n-dimensional space into distinct classes, making it easier to classify new data points in the future. This optimal boundary is known as the hyperplane.

SVM identifies the extreme data points, or vectors, that assist in defining the hyperplane. These critical points are referred to as support vectors, which is how the algorithm gets its name—Support Vector Machine.

Consider the below diagram in which there are two different categories that are classified using a decision boundary or hyperplane:

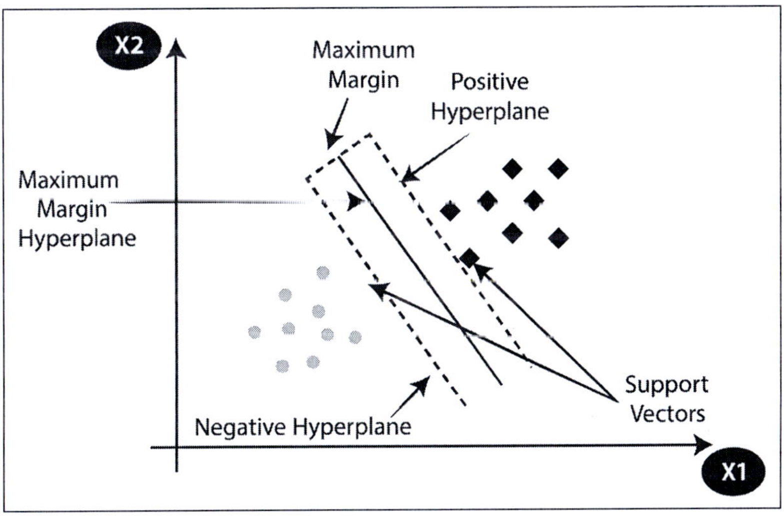

Figure 1.7: *Support Vector Machine*

SVM algorithms can be used for **Face detection, image classification, text categorization,** etc.

Hyperplane and Support Vectors in the SVM algorithm Hyperplane

There can be multiple lines/decision boundaries to segregate the classes in n-dimensional space, but we need to find out the best decision boundary that helps to classify the data points. This best boundary is known as the hyperplane of SVM.

The dimensions of the hyperplane depend on the features present in the dataset, which means if there are 2 features (as shown in image), then the hyperplane will be a straight line. And if there are 3 features, then the hyperplane will be a 2-dimension plane. We always create a hyperplane that has a maximum margin, which means the maximum distance between the data points.

Support Vectors

The data points or vectors that are the closest to the hyperplane and which affect the position of the hyperplane are termed as Support Vectors. These vectors support the hyperplane, hence called a Support vector.

Types of SVM

- **Linear SVM:** Linear SVM is used for linearly separable data, which means if a dataset can be classified into two classes by using a single straight line, then such data is termed as linearly separable data, and classifier is used called as Linear SVM classifier.
- **Non-linear SVM:** Non-Linear SVM is used for non-linearly separated data, which means if a dataset cannot be classified by using a straight line, then such data is termed as non-linear data and classifier used is called as Non-linear SVM classifier.

Linear SVM

The working of the SVM algorithm can be understood by using an example. Suppose we have a dataset that has two tags, and the dataset has two features x1 and x2. We want a classifier that can classify the pair(x1, x2) of coordinates in either green or blue. So as it is 2-d space so by just using a straight line, we can easily separate these two classes. But there can be multiple lines that can separate these classes. Consider the below image:

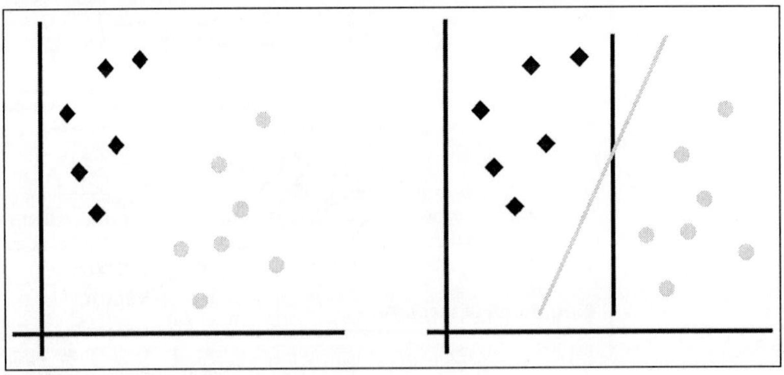

Figure 1.8: *Linearly separable data points*

The SVM algorithm helps to find the best line or decision boundary; this best boundary or region is called a **hyperplane**. SVM algorithm finds the closest point of the lines from both the classes. These points are called support vectors. The distance between the vectors and the hyperplane is called the margin. And the goal of SVM is to maximize this margin. The **hyperplane** with maximum margin is called the **optimal hyperplane**.

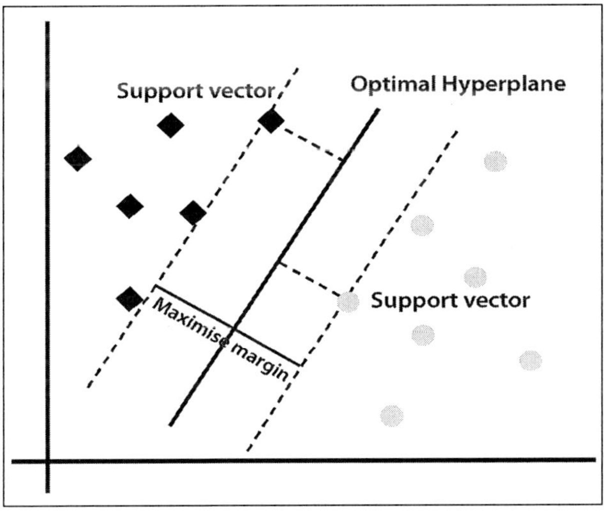

Figure 1.9: *Linear SVM*

Non-Linear SVM

If data is linearly arranged, then we can separate it by using a straight line, but for non-linear data, we cannot draw a single straight line. Consider the below image:

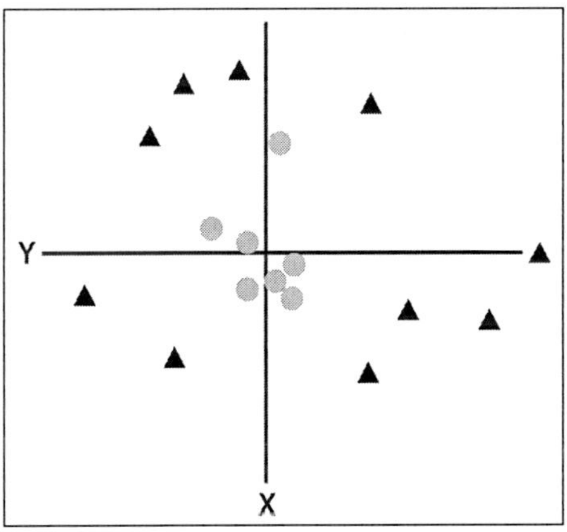

Figure 1.10: *Non linearly separable data points*

So to separate these data points, we need to add one more dimension. For linear data, we have used two dimensions x and y, so for non-linear data, we will add a third-dimension z. It can be calculated as:

$$z = x^2 + y^2$$

By adding the third dimension, the sample space will become as below image:

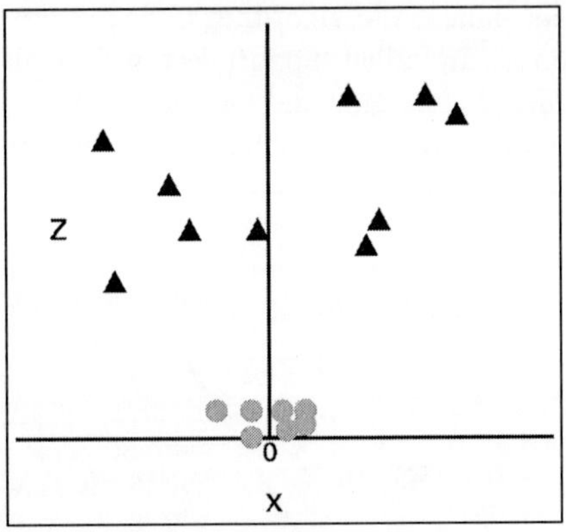

***Figure 1.11**: Adding dimension to separate data points*

So now, SVM will divide the datasets into classes in the following way. Consider the below image:

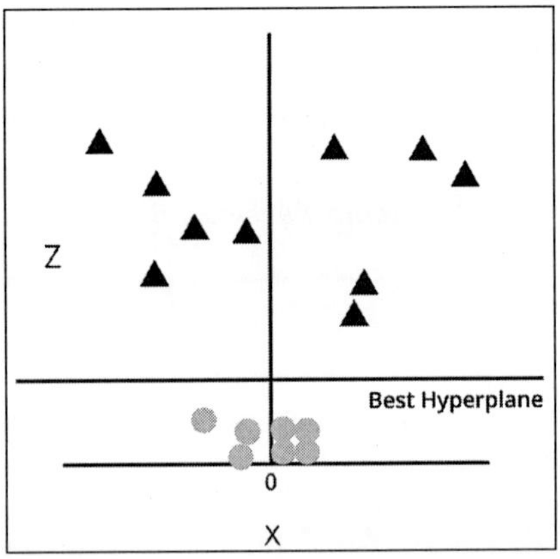

***Figure 1.12**: Non Linear SVM - finding best hyper plane*

Since we are in 3-d Space, hence it is looking like a plane parallel to the x-axis. If we convert it in 2d space with z = 1, then it will become as:

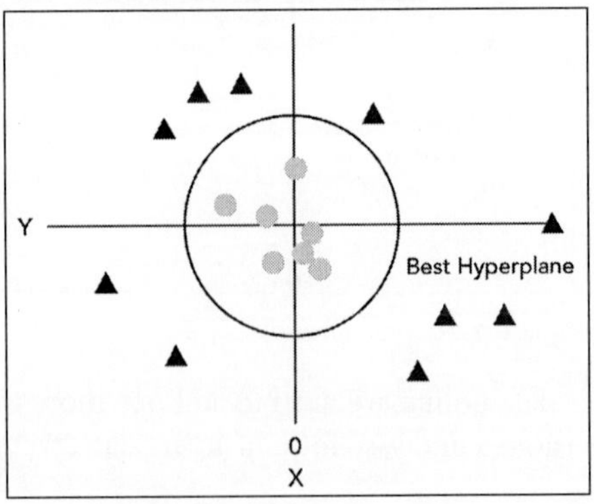

***Figure 1.13:** Non Linear SVM*

Hence we get a circumference of radius 1 in case of non-linear data.

1.2.2 Perceptron

The Perceptron is a machine learning algorithm used for supervised learning, specifically for binary classification tasks. It is also known as an artificial neuron or neural network unit that assists in detecting specific input data computations, particularly in business intelligence. The Perceptron model is considered one of the simplest and most effective types of artificial neural networks. As a supervised learning algorithm for binary classification, it can be viewed as a single-layer neural network with four key components: input values, weights and bias, net sum, and an activation function.

The Perceptron model, developed by Mr. Frank Rosenblatt, serves as a binary classifier and consists of three main components, which are outlined below:

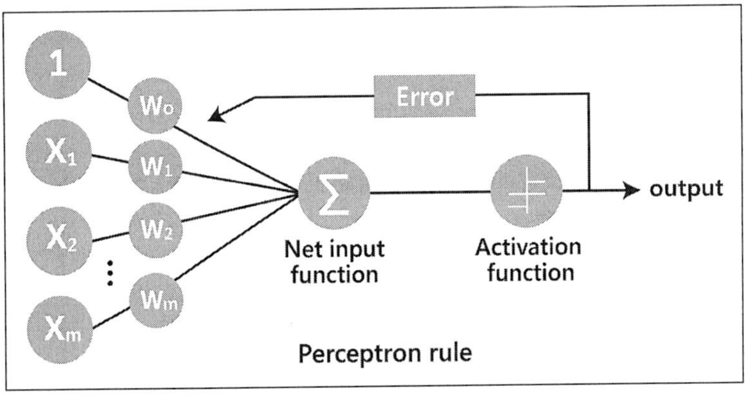

Figure 1.14: *Perceptron*

- **Input Nodes or Input Layer:** This is the primary component of Perceptron which accepts the initial data into the system for further processing. Each input node contains a real numerical value.
- **Weight and Bias:** Weight parameter represents the strength of the connection between units. This is another most important parameter of Perceptron components. Weight is directly proportional to the strength of the associated input neuron in deciding the output. Further, Bias can be considered as the line of intercept in a linear equation.
- **Activation Function:** These are the final and important components that help to determine whether the neuron will fire or not. Activation Function can be considered primarily as a step function.

Types of Activation Functions

- Sign function
- Step function, and
- Sigmoid function

The data scientist uses the activation function to make subjective decisions based on different problem statements, ultimately generating the desired outputs. The choice of activation function can vary (e.g., Sign, Step, and Sigmoid) in perceptron models, depending on factors such as the learning process's speed and whether there are vanishing or exploding gradients.

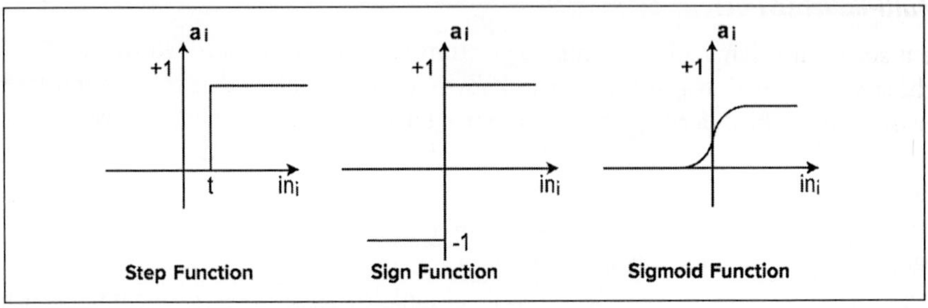

Figure 1.15: *Activation Functions*

In Machine Learning, a perceptron is regarded as a single-layer neural network consisting of four key parameters: input values (input nodes), weights and bias, net sum, and the activation function. The perceptron model starts by multiplying all input values by their respective weights, then summing these weighted values to produce the weighted sum. This sum is then passed through the activation function 'f' to produce the output. The activation function, often called the step function, is denoted by **'f'**.

The step function, or activation function, plays a crucial role in mapping the output to the required range, such as (0,1) or (-1,1). It's important to understand that the weight of an input indicates the strength of the node, while the input's bias value allows for shifting the activation function curve up or down.

Perceptron model works in two important steps as follows:

Step 1: In the first step first, multiply all input values with corresponding weight values and then add them to determine the weighted sum. Mathematically, we can calculate the weighted sum as follows:

$$\sum w_i{}^*x_i = x_1{}^*w_1 + x_2{}^*w_2 + \ldots w_n{}^*x_n$$

Add a special term called **bias 'b'** to this weighted sum to improve the model's performance.

$$\sum w_i{}^*x_i + \mathbf{b}$$

Step 2: In the second step, an activation function is applied with the above- mentioned weighted sum, which gives us output either in binary form or a continuous value as follows:

$$\mathbf{Y = f(\sum w_i{}^*x_i + b)}$$

Types of Perceptron Models

Based on the layers, Perceptron models are divided into two types. These are as follows:

1. Single-layer Perceptron Model
2. Multi-layer Perceptron Model

1. Single Layer Perceptron Model

This is one of the easiest Artificial neural networks (ANN) types. A single- layered perceptron model consists of a feed-forward network and also includes a threshold transfer function inside the model. The main objective of the single- layer perceptron model is to analyze the linearly separable objects with binary outcomes.

"Single-layer perceptrons can learn only linearly separable patterns."

2. Multi-Layered Perceptron Model

Like a single-layer perceptron model, a multi-layer perceptron model also has the same model structure but has a greater number of hidden layers which executes in two stages as follows:

- **Forward Stage:** Activation functions start from the input layer in the forward stage and terminate on the output layer.
- **Backward Stage:** In the backward stage, weight and bias values are modified as per the model's requirement. In this stage, the error between actual output and demanded originated backward on the output layer and ended on the input layer.

A multi-layer perceptron model has greater processing power and can process linear and non-linear patterns. Further, it can also implement logic gates such as AND, OR, XOR, NAND, NOT, XNOR, NOR.

Advantages of Multi-Layer Perceptron

- A multi-layered perceptron model can be used to solve complex non- linear problems.
- It works well with both small and large input data.
- It helps us to obtain quick predictions after the training.
- It helps to obtain the same accuracy ratio with large as well as small data.

Disadvantages of Multi-Layer Perceptron

- In Multi-layer perceptron, computations are difficult and time-consuming.
- In multi-layer Perceptron, it is difficult to predict how much the dependent variable affects each independent variable.
- The model functioning depends on the quality of the training.

Characteristics of Perceptron

1. Perceptron is a machine learning algorithm for supervised learning of binary classifiers.
2. In Perceptron, the weight coefficient is automatically learned.
3. Initially, weights are multiplied with input features, and the decision is made whether the neuron is fired or not.
4. The activation function applies a step rule to check whether the weight function is greater than zero.
5. The linear decision boundary is drawn, enabling the distinction between the two linearly separable classes +1 and -1.
6. If the added sum of all input values is more than the threshold value, it must have an output signal; otherwise, no output will be shown.

1.2.3 Logistic Regression

Logistic regression is a widely used machine learning algorithm that falls under supervised learning. It is employed for predicting a categorical dependent variable based on a set of independent variables. Logistic regression is specifically used to predict the outcome of a categorical dependent variable, meaning the result must be a discrete or categorical value such as Yes/No, 0/1, or True/False. Rather than providing exact values of 0 or 1, **it generates**

probabilistic values between 0 and 1. While logistic regression is similar to linear regression, the key difference lies in their applications. Linear regression is used for solving regression problems, **whereas logistic regression is applied to classification problems.**

In logistic regression, instead of fitting a regression line, an "S" shaped logistic function is used, which predicts two possible outcomes (0 or 1). The logistic curve represents the probability of an event occurring, such as whether cells are cancerous or whether a mouse is obese based on its weight.

Logistic regression is an important algorithm in machine learning due to its ability to provide probabilities and classify new data using both continuous and discrete datasets. It can classify observations effectively across various types of data and is capable of identifying the most influential variables for classification. The image below illustrates the logistic function:

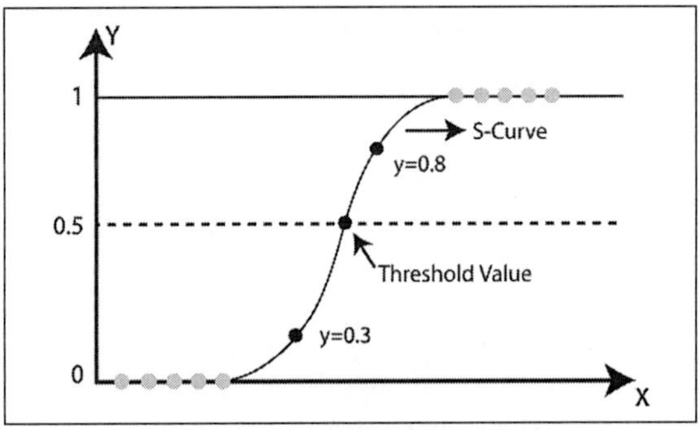

Figure 1.16: *Logistic Regression*

Logistic Regression Equation

The Logistic regression equation can be obtained from the Linear Regression equation. The mathematical steps to get Logistic Regression equations are given below:

- We know the equation of the straight line can be written as:

$$y = b_o + b_1x_1 + b_2x_2 + b_3x_3 + \cdots + b_nx_n$$

- In Logistic Regression y can be between 0 and 1 only, so for this let's divide the above equation by (1-y):

$$\frac{y}{1-y}\text{; 0 for y=0, and infinity for y=1}$$

- But we need range between -[infinity] to +[infinity], then take logarithm of the equation it will become:

$$\log\left[\frac{y}{1-y}\right] = b_0 + b_1x_1 + b_2x_2 + b_3x_3 + \ldots + b_nx_n$$

The above equation is the final equation for Logistic Regression.

Type of Logistic Regression

On the basis of the categories, Logistic Regression can be classified into three types:

- **Binomial:** In binomial Logistic regression, there can be only two possible types of the dependent variables, such as 0 or 1, Pass or Fail, etc.

- **Multinomial:** In multinomial Logistic regression, there can be 3 or more possible unordered types of the dependent variable, such as "cat", "dogs", or "sheep"
- **Ordinal:** In ordinal Logistic regression, there can be 3 or more possible ordered types of dependent variables, such as "low", "Medium", or "High".

1.3 INTRODUCTION TO NEURAL NETWORK

A neural network is **a method in artificial intelligence that teaches computers to process data in a way that is inspired by the human brain**. It is a type of machine learning process, called deep learning, that uses interconnected nodes or neurons in a layered structure that resembles the human brain.

Different types of Neural Networks in Deep Learning

There are three important types of neural networks that form the basis for most pre-trained models in deep learning:

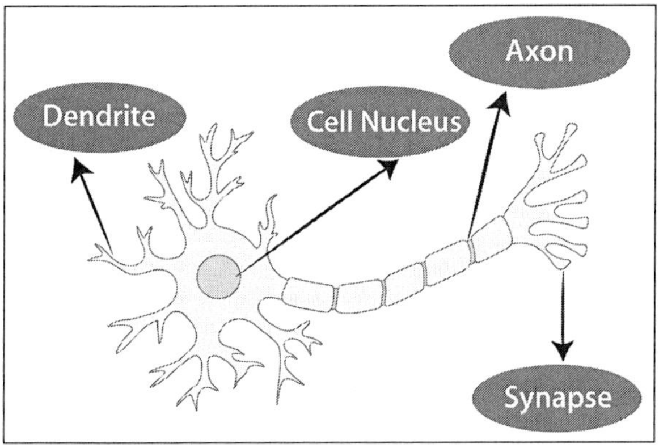

Figure 1.17: Neural Networks in Deep Learning

- Artificial Neural Networks (ANN)
- Convolution Neural Networks (CNN)
- Recurrent Neural Networks (RNN)

Artificial Neural Networks

The term "**Artificial Neural Network**" is derived from Biological neural networks that develop the structure of a human brain. Similar to the human brain that has neurons interconnected to one another, artificial neural networks also have neurons that are interconnected to one another in various layers of the networks.

Biological Neural Network	Artificial Neural Network
Dendrites	Inputs
Cell nucleus	Nodes
Synapse	Weights
Axon	Output

Convolution Neural Network (CNN)

Convolution neural networks contain a three-dimensional arrangement of neurons, instead of the standard two-dimensional array. The first layer is called a convolutional layer. Each neuron in the convolutional layer only processes the information from a small part of the visual field. Input features are taken batch-wise like a filter. The network understands the images in parts and can compute these operations multiple times to complete the full image processing. Processing involves conversion of the image from RGB or HSI scale to grey-scale. Furthering the changes in the pixel value will help to detect the edges and images can be classified into different categories.

Recurrent Neural Network (RNN)

Recurrent Neural Networks are a type of Neural Network where the output from the previous step is fed as input to the current step. In traditional neural networks, all the inputs and outputs are independent of each other, but in cases like when it is required to predict the next word of a sentence, the previous words are required and hence there is a need to remember the previous words.

Architecture of Neural Network

A simple neural network consists of three components :

- Input layer
- Hidden layer
- Output layer

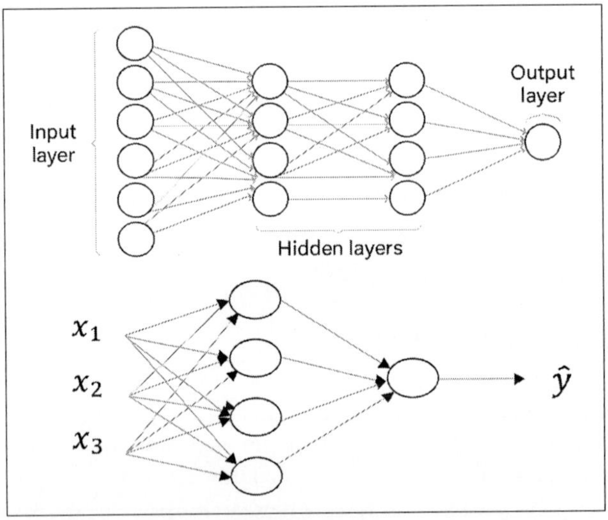

***Figure 1.18:** Architecture of Neural Network*

- **Input Layer:** Also known as Input nodes are the inputs/information from the outside world is provided to the model to learn and derive conclusions from. Input nodes pass the information to the next layer i.e. Hidden layer.
- **Hidden Layer:** Hidden layer is the set of neurons where all the computations are performed on the input data. There can be any number of hidden layers in a neural network. The simplest network consists of a single hidden layer.

- **Output layer:** The output layer is the output/conclusions of the model derived from all the computations performed. There can be single or multiple nodes in the output layer. If we have a binary classification problem the output node is 1 but in the case of multiclass classification, the output nodes can be more than 1.

1.4 WHAT A SHALLOW NETWORK COMPUTES

"Shallow" neural networks is **a term used to describe NN that usually have only one hidden layer** as opposed to deep NN which have several hidden layers, often of various types. Shallow neural networks consist of only 1 or 2 hidden layers. Understanding a shallow neural network gives us an insight into what exactly is going on inside a deep neural network. In this post, let us see what is a shallow neural network and its working in a mathematical context. The figure below shows a shallow neural network with 1 hidden layer, 1 input layer and 1 output layer.

The Neuron

The neuron is the atomic unit of a neural network. Given an input, it provides the output and passes that output as an input to the subsequent layer. A neuron can be thought of as a combination of 2 parts:

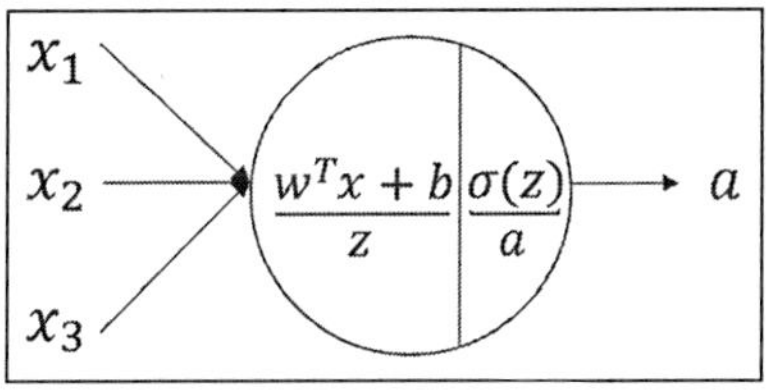

Figure 1.19: *Shallow Network*

- The first part computes the output **Z**, using the inputs and the weights.
- The second part performs the activation on **Z** to give out the final output **A** of the neuron.

The Hidden Layer

The hidden layer comprises various neurons, each of which performs the above 2 calculations. The 4 neurons present in the hidden layer of our shallow neural network compute the following:

$$z_1^{[1]} = w_1^{[1]T}x + b_1^{[1]}, a_1^{[1]} = \sigma\left(z_1^{[1]}\right)$$
$$z_2^{[1]} = w_2^{[1]T}x + b_2^{[1]}, a_2^{[1]} = \sigma\left(z_2^{[1]}\right)$$
$$z_3^{[1]} = w_3^{[1]T}x + b_3^{[1]}, a_3^{[1]} = \sigma\left(z_3^{[1]}\right)$$
$$z_4^{[1]} = w_4^{[1]T}x + b_4^{[1]}, a_4^{[1]} = \sigma\left(z_4^{[1]}\right)$$

In the above equations,

1. The superscript number *[i]* denotes the layer number and the subscript number ***j*** denotes the neuron number in a particular layer.
2. *X* is the input vector consisting of 3 features.

3. *W[i]j* is the weight associated with neuron ***j*** present in the layer ***i***.
4. *b[i]j* is the bias associated with neuron ***j*** present in the layer ***i***.
5. *Z[i]j* is the intermediate output associated with neuron ***j*** present in the layer ***i***.
6. *A[i]j* is the final output associated with neuron ***j*** present in the layer ***i***.
7. *Sigma* is the sigmoid activation function. Mathematically it is defined as:

$$\sigma(x) = \frac{1}{1 + e^{-x}}$$

As we can see, the above 4 equations seem redundant. Therefore we will vectorize them as:

1.5 TRAINING A NETWORK

1. **Pick a neural network architecture:** This implies that you shall be pondering primarily upon the connectivity patterns of the neural network including some of the following aspects:

$$Z^{[1]} = X^{[1]T}X + b^{[1]}$$

$$A^{[1]} = \sigma\left(Z^{[1]}\right)$$

   - **Number of input nodes**: The way to identify the number of input nodes is to identify the number of features.
   - **Number of hidden layers**: The default is to use the single or one hidden layer. This is the most common practice.
   - **Number of nodes in each of the hidden layers**: In case of using multiple hidden layers, the best practice is to use the same number of nodes in each hidden layer. In general practice, the number of hidden units is taken as a comparable number to that of the number of input nodes. That means one could take either the same number of hidden nodes as input nodes or maybe twice or thrice the number of input nodes.
   - **Number of output nodes**: The way to identify number of output nodes is to identify the number of output classes you want the neural network to process.
2. **Random Initialization of Weights:** The weights are randomly initialized to value in between 0 and 1, or rather, very close to zero.
3. Implementation of forward propagation algorithm to calculate hypothesis function for a set of input vectors for any of the hidden layers.
4. Implementation of cost function for optimizing parameter values. One may recall that cost function would help determine how well the neural network fits the training data.
5. Implementation of back propagation algorithm to compute the error vector related with each of the nodes.
6. Use gradient checking method to compare the gradient calculated using partial derivatives of cost function using back propagation and using numerical estimate of cost function gradient. The gradient checking method is used to validate if the implementation of the backpropagation method is correct.
7. Use gradient descent or advanced optimization technique with back propagation to try and minimize the cost function as a function of parameters or weights.

1.6 LOSS FUNCTION

The loss function in a neural network **quantifies the difference between the expected outcome and the outcome produced by the machine learning model**. From the loss function, we can derive the gradients which are used to update the weights. The average over all losses constitutes the cost. Loss functions are divided into two categories.

1. Regression loss
2. Classification Loss – Binary and Multi-class Classification

Regression Loss

1. Mean Squared Error (MSE)

Squared Error loss for each training example, also known as **L2 Loss**, is the square of the difference between the actual and the predicted values:

$$MSE = \frac{1}{N}\sum_{t=1}^{N}(y_i - \breve{y})^2$$

2. Mean Squared Logarithmic Error (MSLE)

It measures the ratio between actual and predicted using logarithmic values. It is a good choice to predict the continuous data.

$$MSLE = \frac{1}{n}\sum_{i=1}^{n}(\log(y_i) - \log)^2$$

3. Mean Absolute Error (MAE)

Absolute Error for each training example is the distance between the predicted and the actual values, irrespective of the sign. Absolute Error is also known as the **L1 loss:**

$$MAE = \frac{\sum_{i=1}^{n} |y_i - \hat{y}_i|}{n}$$

Binary Classification Loss Functions

1. Binary Cross Entropy Loss

Entropy indicates disorder or uncertainty. It is measured for a random variable X with probability distribution p(X): Cross-entropy is the default loss function to use for binary classification problems. It is intended for use with binary classification where the target values are in the set {0, 1}.

2. Hinge Loss

An alternative to cross-entropy for binary classification problems is the hinge loss function, primarily developed for use with Support Vector Machine (SVM) models. It is intended for use with binary classification where the target values are in the set {-1, 1}.

3. Squared Hinge Loss

It is an extension of Hinge Loss. It is mainly used for categorical prediction or yes/no kind of decision problems.

Multi-Class Classification Loss Functions

Multi-Class classification are those predictive modeling problems where examples are assigned one of more than two classes.

1. Multiclass Cross Entropy Loss

Cross-entropy is the default loss function to use for multi-class classification problems. In this case, it is intended for use with multi-class classification where the target values are in the set {0, 1, 3, …, n}, where each class is assigned a unique integer value. It is best loss function for text classification.

2. Sparse Multiclass Cross-Entropy Loss

Sparse cross-entropy addresses the same performance as cross-entropy calculation of error and it is mainly used to handle large amount of data.

1.7 BACKPROPAGATION

Feedforward Neural Network

A feedforward neural network is an artificial neural network where the nodes never form a cycle. This kind of neural network has an input layer, hidden layers, and an output layer. It is the first and simplest type of artificial neural network.

Backpropagation

Backpropagation is the essence of neural network training. It is the feedforward network with feedback. It is the method of fine-tuning the weights of a neural network based on the error rate obtained in the previous epoch (i.e., iteration). Proper tuning of the weights allows you to reduce error rates and make the model reliable by increasing its generalization.

Backpropagation in a neural network is a short form for "backward propagation of errors." It is a standard method of training artificial neural networks. This method helps calculate the gradient of a loss function with respect to all the weights in the network.

The Backpropagation algorithm in a neural network computes the gradient of the loss function for a single weight by the chain rule. It efficiently computes one layer at a time, unlike a native direct computation. It computes the gradient, but it does not define how the gradient is used. It generalizes the computation in the delta rule.

Backpropagation Algorithm

1. Inputs X, arrive through the preconnected path
2. Input is modelled using real weights W. The weights are usually randomly selected.
3. Calculate the output for every neuron from the input layer, to the hidden layers, to the output layer.
4. Calculate the error in the outputs

5. Error = Actual Output – Desired Output
6. Travel back from the output layer to the hidden layer to adjust the weights such that the error is decreased.

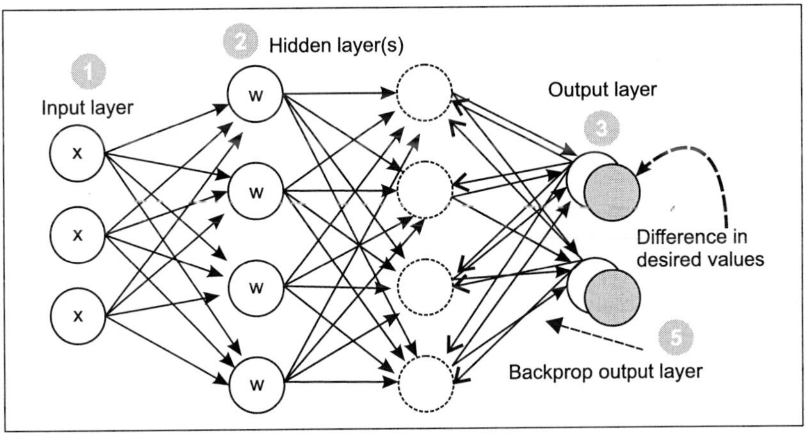

Figure 1.20: *Backpropagation*

1.8 STOCHASTIC GRADIENT DESCENT

Gradient descent is an optimization algorithm which is commonly-used to train machine learning models and neural networks. Optimization algorithm refers to the task of minimizing/maximizing an objective function f(x) parameterized by x. Similarly, in machine learning, optimization is the task of minimizing the cost function parameterized by the model's parameters. The main objective of gradient descent is to minimize the convex function using iteration of parameter updates. It helps in finding the local minimum of a function.

The best way to define the local minimum or local maximum of a function using gradient descent is as follows:

- If we move towards a negative gradient or away from the gradient of the function at the current point, it will give the **local minimum** of that function.

Whenever we move towards a positive gradient or towards the gradient of the function at the current point, we will get the **local maximum** of that function.

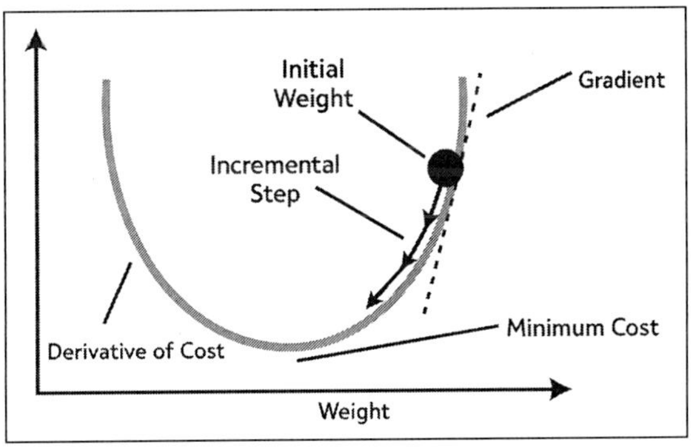

Figure 1.21: *Gradient Descent*

Types of Gradient Descent

Typically, there are three types of Gradient Descent

1. Batch Gradient Descent
2. Stochastic Gradient Descent
3. Mini-batch Gradient Descent

Stochastic Gradient Descent (SGD)

The word 'stochastic' means a system or a process that is linked with a random probability. Hence, in Stochastic Gradient Descent, a few samples are selected randomly instead of the whole data set for each iteration. In Gradient Descent, there is a term called "batch" which denotes the total number of samples from a dataset that is used for calculating the gradient for each iteration. In typical Gradient Descent optimization, like Batch Gradient Descent, the batch is taken to be the whole dataset. Although, using the whole dataset is really useful for getting to the minima in a less noisy and less random manner, the problem arises when our datasets get big. Suppose, you have a million samples in your dataset, so if you use a typical Gradient Descent optimization technique, you will have to use all of the one million samples for completing one iteration while performing the Gradient Descent, and it has to be done for every iteration until the minima is reached. Hence, it becomes computationally very expensive to perform.

Advantages

- Good Efficiency.
- Ease of implementation.

Disadvantages

- It requires a number of hyper parameters such as the regularization parameter and the number of iterations.
- It is sensitive to feature scaling.

1.9 NEURAL NETS AS UNIVERSAL FUNCTION APPROXIMATES

Neural network architecture aims at finding any mathematical function y= f(x) that can map attributes(x) to output(y). The accuracy of this function i.e. mapping differs depending on the distribution of the dataset and the architecture of the network employed. The function f(x) can be arbitrarily complex. The Universal Approximation Theorem tells us that Neural Networks has a kind of universality i.e. no matter what f(x) is, there is a network that can approximately approach the result and do the job! This result holds for any number of inputs and outputs.

UNIT 2

Introduction to Deep Learning

2.1 HISTORY OF DEEP LEARNING [DL]

1. The chain rule that underlies the back-propagation algorithm was invented in the seventeenth century.
2. Beginning in the 1940s, the function approximation techniques were used to motivate machine learning models such as the perceptron.
3. The earliest models were based on linear models. Critics including Marvin Minsky pointed out several of the flaws of the linear model family, such as its inability to learn the XOR function, which led to a backlash against the entire neural network approach.
4. Efficient applications of the chain rule based on dynamic programming began to appear in the 1960s and 1970s.
5. Werbos (1981) proposed applying chain rule techniques for training artificial neural networks. The idea was finally developed in practice after being independently rediscovered in different ways
6. Following the success of back-propagation, neural network research gained popularity and reached a peak in the early 1990s. Afterwards, other machine learning techniques became more popular until the modern deep learning techniques that began in 2006.
7. The core ideas behind modern feedforward networks have not changed substantially since the 1980s. The same back-propagation algorithm and the same approaches to gradient descent are still in use.

Most of the improvement in neural network performance from 1986 to 2015 can be attributed to two factors. First, larger datasets have reduced the degree to which statistical generalization is a challenge for neural networks. Second, neural networks have become much larger, because of more powerful computers and better software infrastructure. A small number of algorithmic changes have also improved the performance of neural networks noticeably. One of these algorithmic changes were the replacement of mean squared error with the cross-entropy family of loss functions. Mean squared error was popular in the 1980s and 1990s but was gradually replaced by cross-entropy losses and the principle of maximum likelihood as ideas spread between the statistics community and the machine learning community.

The other major algorithmic change that has greatly improved the performance of feed forward networks was the replacement of sigmoid hidden units with piecewise linear hidden units, such as rectified linear units. Rectification using the max{0, z} function was introduced in early neural network models and dates back at least as far as the Cognitron and Neocognitron.

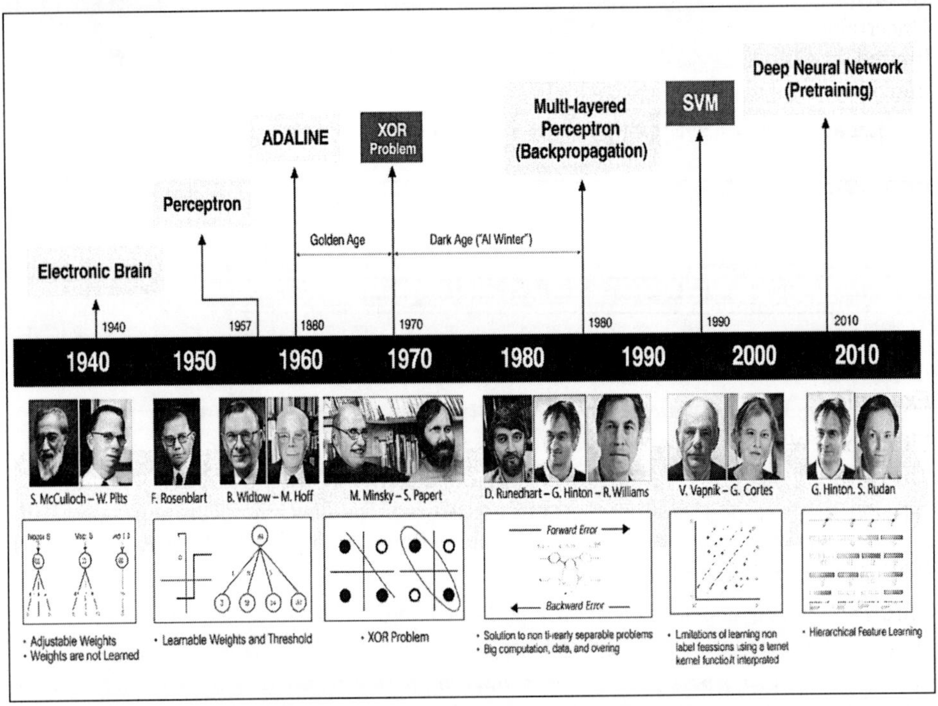

Figure 2.1: *History of Deep Learning [DL]*

Random weights are sufficient to propagate useful information through a rectified linear network, enabling the classifier layer at the top to learn how to map different feature vectors to class identities. When more data is available, learning begins to extract enough useful knowledge to exceed the performance of randomly chosen parameters.

When the modern resurgence of deep learning began in 2006, feedforward networks continued to have a bad reputation. From about 2006 to 2012, it was widely believed that feedforward networks would not perform well unless they were assisted by other models, such as probabilistic models.

Today, it is now known that with the right resources and engineering practices, feedforward networks perform very well. Today, gradient-based learning in feedforward networks is used as a tool to develop probabilistic models. Feedforward networks continue to have unfulfilled potential.

2.2 A PROBABILISTIC THEORY OF DEEP LEARNING

Probability is the science of quantifying uncertain things. Most machine learning and deep learning systems utilize a lot of data to learn about patterns in the data. Whenever data is utilized in a system rather than sole logic, uncertainty grows up and whenever uncertainty grows up, probability becomes relevant.

By introducing probability to a deep learning system, we introduce common sense to the system. In deep learning, several models like Bayesian models, probabilistic graphical models, Hidden Markov models are used. They depend entirely on probability concepts.

Probabilistic Theory – ACTING UNDER UNCERTAINTY

Uncertainty is a situation which involves imperfect and/or unknown information. Uncertainty arises in partially observable and/or stochastic environments. A state of having limited knowledge where it is impossible to exactly describe the existing state, a future outcome, or more than one possible outcome.

Let action A_t = leave for airport t minutes before flight. Will A_t get me there on time?

Problems

- partial observability (road state, other drivers' plans, etc.)
- noisy sensors (traffic reports)
- uncertainty in action outcomes (flat tire, etc.)
- immense complexity of modeling and predicting traffic

Example 1

Flip a coin. What is the chance of it landing heads side up? There are 2 sides, heads and tails. The heads side is one of them, thus

(Heads) = 1/(1+1) = ½ = .50 = 50%

Example 2

Throw a die. What is the probability of getting a 3. P(die = 3) = 1 side with a 3 / 6 sides

P(die = 3) = 1/6 = .167 = 16.7%

Conditional Probability

Events A and B are events that are not mutually exclusive, but occur conditionally on the occurrence of one another.

The probability that event A will occur: p(A)

Probability of A

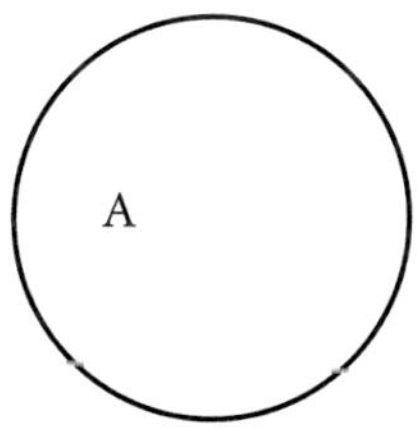

The probability that event B will occur: p(B)

Probability of B

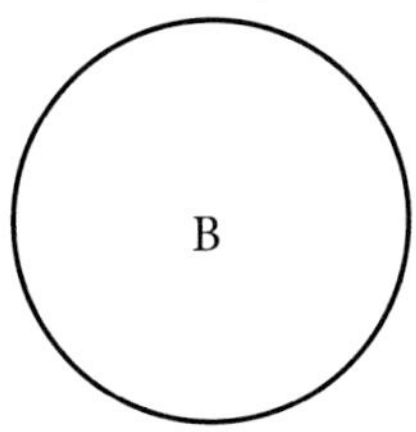

The number of times that both A and B occur or the probability that both events A and B will occur is called the **joint probability.**

Mathematically joint probability is defined as: $p(A \cap B)$

i.e. the probability that both A and B will occur

Joint probability of A and B

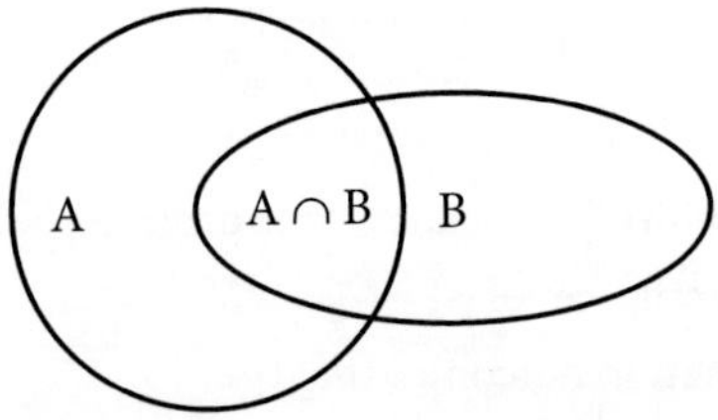

Figure 2.2: *Joint Probability*

The probability that event A will occur if event B occurs is called **conditional probability.**

$$P(A \mid B) = \frac{\text{the number of times A and B can occur}}{\text{the number of times B can occur}}$$

or

$$P(A \mid B) = \frac{P(A \cap B)}{P(B)}$$

Let's take an example.

Suppose we have 2 dice and we want to know what the probability of getting an 8 is. Normally if we roll both at the same time the probability is 5/36.

1,1	1,2	1,3	1,4	1,5	1,6
2,1	2,2	2,3	2,4	2,5	2,6
3,1	3,2	3,3	3,4	3,5	3,6
4,1	4,2	4,3	4,4	4,5	4,6
5,1	5,2	5,3	5,4	5,5	5,6
6,1	6,2	6,3	6,4	6,5	6,6

But what happens if we roll the first die and get a 5, now what is the probability of getting an 8?

There is only one way to get an 8 after a 5 has been rolled. You have to roll a 3. Looking at the formula:

$$P(A|B) = \frac{P(A \cap B)}{P(B)}$$

Lets rephrase it for our problem

P(getting an 8 using 2 die | given that we roll a 5 with first dice)

$$= \frac{P(\text{rolling 5 and 3})}{P(\text{rolling a 5})}$$

$P(A|B) = (1/36) / (1/6) = (1/36) * (6/1) = 6/36 = 1/6$

Bayes's Rule

The below equation is Bayes rule:

$$P(B|A) = \frac{P(A|B)P(B)}{P(A)}$$

Bayes rule allows unknown probabilities to be computed from known conditional probabilities.

In the given bayes rule equation,

- Events A, B – Hypothesis
- P(B|A) – **Posterior probability** (updated probability after the evidence is considered)
- P(A|B) – **Conditional Probability** or **Likelihood** (probability of the evidence, given the belief is true)
- P(B) – **Prior probability** (the probability before the evidence is considered)
- P(A) – **Marginal probability** (probability of the evidence, under any circumstance)

Example 1

A bag I contains 4 white and 6 black balls while another Bag II contains 4 white and 3 black balls. One ball is drawn at random from one of the bags, and it is found to be black. Find the probability that it was drawn from Bag I.

Solution

Let E1 - the event of choosing bag I, E2 - the event of choosing bag II

A - the event of drawing a black ball.

By using Bayes' theorem, the probability of drawing a black ball from bag I out of two bags,

$$\mathbf{P(E1/A) = \frac{P(A/E1)P(E1)}{P(A)}}$$

P(E1) = P(E2) = ½

P(A/E1) = P(drawing a black ball from Bag I) = 6/10 = 3/5 P(A/E2) = P(drawing a black ball from Bag II) = 3/7

P(A) = P(E1) P(A/E1) + P(E2) P(A/E2) = 18/35

$$\mathbf{P(E1/A) = \frac{P(A/E1)P(E1)}{P(A)} = 7/12}$$

Naive Bayes Classifier

- Naive Bayes algorithm is a supervised learning algorithm, which is based on **Bayes theorem** and used for solving classification problems.
- It is mainly used in text classification that includes a high-dimensional training dataset.
- Naive Bayes Classifier is one of the simple and most effective Classification algorithms which helps in building the fast machine learning models that can make quick predictions.

- It is a probabilistic classifier, which means it predicts on the basis of the probability of an object.
- Some popular examples of Naïve Bayes Algorithm are spam filtration, Sentimental analysis, and classifying articles.

Advantages of Naive Bayes Classifier

- Naive Bayes is one of the fast and easy ML algorithms to predict a class of datasets.
- It can be used for Binary as well as Multi-class Classifications.
- It is the most popular choice for **text classification problems.**

Disadvantages of Naive Bayes Classifier

- Naive Bayes assumes that all features are independent or unrelated, so it cannot learn the relationship between features.

Applications of Naive Bayes Classifier

- It is used for **Credit Scoring.**
- It is used in **medical data classification.**
- It can be used in **real-time predictions.**
- It is used in Text classification such as **Spam filtering.**

Example

We want to use Bayes theorem to find out the likelihood of playing tennis for a given set of weather attributes. The attribute values (Outlook, Temperature, Humidity, and Wind).

To determine our answer (if we are going to play tennis given a certain set of conditions) we make an expression that determines the probability based on our training examples from the table. Given a = (Outlook = sunny, Temperature = cool, Humidity = high, Wind = strong) to be selected.

Day	Outlook	Temperature	Humidity	Wind	Play Tennis
1	Sunny	Hot	High	Weak	No
2	Sunny	Hot	High	Strong	No
3	Overcast	Hot	High	Weak	Yes
4	Rain	Mild	High	Weak	Yes
5	Rain	Cool	Normal	Weak	Yes
6	Rain	Cool	Normal	Strong	No
7	Overcast	Cool	Normal	Strong	Yes
8	Sunny	Mild	High	Weak	No
9	Sunny	Cool	Normal	Weak	Yes
10	Rain	Mild	Normal	Weak	Yes
11	Sunny	Mild	Normal	Strong	Yes
12	Overcast	Mild	High	Strong	Yes

Day	Outlook	Temperature	Humidity	Wind	Play Tennis
13	Overcast	Hot	Normal	Weak	Yes
14	Rain	Mild	High	Strong	No

$$P(\text{Play Tennis} \mid \text{Attributes}) = \frac{P(\text{Attributes} \mid \text{Play Tennis}) * P(\text{Play Tennis})}{P(\text{Attributes})}$$

P(a|v) = P(Outlook, Temperature, Humidity, Wind | Play tennis, Don't Play tennis)

First we estimate the probability of playing tennis:

P(Play Tennis = Yes) = 9/14 = .64 P(Play Tennis = No) = 5/14 = .36

Then we estimate the conditional probabilities of the individual attributes

Outlook

- P(Outlook = Sunny | Play Tennis = Yes) = 2/9 = 0.22
- P(Outlook = Sunny | Play Tennis = No) = 3/5 = 0.6
- P(Outlook = Overcast | Play Tennis = Yes) = 4/9 = 0.44
- P(Outlook = Overcast | Play Tennis = No) = 0/5 = 0
- P(Outlook = Rain | Play Tennis = Yes) = 3/9 = 0.33 P(Outlook = Rain | Play Tennis = No) = 2/5 = 0.4

Temperature

- P(Temperature = Hot | Play Tennis = Yes) = 2/9 = 0.22
- P(Temperature = Hot | Play Tennis = No) = 2/5 = 0.40
- P(Temperature = Mild | Play Tennis = Yes) = 4/9 = 0.44
- P(Temperature = Mild | Play Tennis = No) = 2/5 = 0.40
- P(Temperature = Cool | Play Tennis = Yes) = 3/9 = 0.33 P(Temperature = Cool | Play Tennis = No) = 1/5 = 0.20

Humidity

- P(Humidity = High | Play Tennis = Yes) = 3/9 = 0.33
- P(Humidity = High | Play Tennis = No) = 4/5 = 0.80
- P(Humidity = Normal | Play Tennis = Yes) = 6/9 = 0.66
- P(Humidity = Normal | Play Tennis = No) = 1/5 = 0.20

Wind

- P(Wind = Weak | Play Tennis = Yes) = 6/9 = 0.66
- P(Wind = Weak | Play Tennis = No) = 2/5 = 0.40
- P(Wind = Strong | Play Tennis = Yes) = 3/9 = 0.33
- P(Wind = Strong | Play Tennis = No) = 3/5 = 0.60
- a = (Outlook = sunny, Temperature = cool, Humidity = high, Wind = strong)
- P(Playtennis = No | (Outlook = sunny, Temperature = cool, Humidity = high, Wind = strong))

$$= \frac{P(\text{sunny} \mid \text{Yes}) * P(\text{cool} \mid \text{Yes}) * P(\text{strong} \mid \text{Yes}) * P(\text{yes})}{P(\text{sunn,cool,high,strong}) \mid \text{Yes}) + P(\text{sunny,cool, high,strong})}$$

$$= \frac{(.22 * .33 * .33) * .64}{(.22 * .33 * .33) * .6 * .2 * .8 * .6) * .36}$$

$$= \frac{.0207}{.0051 + .0207}$$

$= \mathbf{0\ .1977}$

$$P(\text{No} \mid (\text{sunny, cool, high, strong})) = \frac{P(\text{sunny,cool,high,strong} \mid \text{No}) * P(\text{No})}{P(\text{sunny,cool,high,strong})}$$

$$= \frac{.0207}{.0051 + .0207}$$

$= \mathbf{0.8023}$

As we can see, the Bayes Naïve classifier gives a value of just about 20% for playing tennis in the described conditions, and a value of 80% for not playing tennis in these conditions, therefore the prediction is that no tennis will be played if the day is like these conditions.

2.3 BACK PROPAGATION NETWORKS (BPN)

Need for Multilayer Networks

- Single Layer networks cannot used to solve Linear Inseparable problems can only be used to solve linear separable problems
- Single layer networks cannot solve complex problems
- Single layer networks cannot be used when large input-output data set is available
- Single layer networks cannot capture the complex information available in the training pairs

Hence to overcome the above said Limitations we use Multi-Layer Networks.

Multi-Layer Networks

- Any neural network which has at least one layer in between input and output layers is called Multi-Layer Networks
- Layers present in between the input and out layers are called Hidden Layers
- Input layer neural unit just collects the inputs and forwards them to the next higher layer
- Hidden layer and output layer neural units process the information's feed to them and produce an appropriate output
- Multi-layer networks provide optimal solution for arbitrary classification problems
- Multi-layer networks use linear discriminants, where the inputs are nonlinear

Back Propagation Networks (BPN)

Introduced by Rumelhart, Hinton, & Williams in 1986.

BPN is a Multi-layer Feedforward Network but error is back propagated, Hence the name Back Propagation Network (BPN). It uses a Supervised Training process; it has a systematic procedure for training the network and is used in Error Detection and Correction.

Generalized Delta Law /Continuous Perceptron Law/ Gradient Descent Law is used in this network. Generalized Delta rule minimizes the mean squared error of the output calculated from the output. Delta law has a faster convergence rate when compared with Perceptron Law.

The Training process used in backpropagation involves three stages, which are listed as below:

1. Feedforward of input training pair
2. Calculation and backpropagation of associated error
3. Adjustments of weights

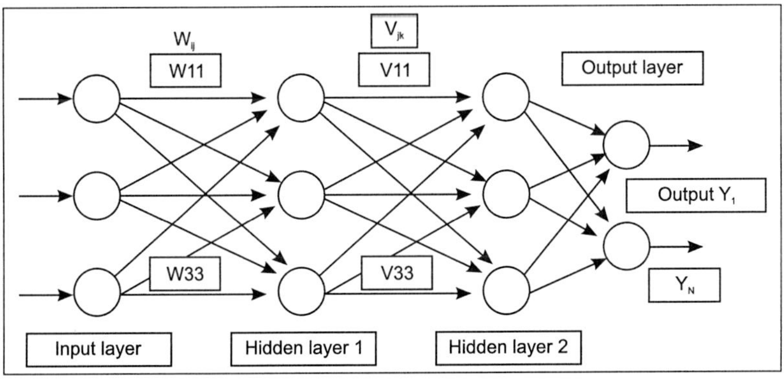

Figure 2.3: *Back Propagation Networks (BPN)*

The algorithm for BPN is as classified int four major steps as follows:

1. Initialization of Bias, Weights
2. Feedforward process
3. Back Propagation of Errors
4. Updating of weights & biases

Algorithm

Step 1: Initialize the weights to small random values near zero.

Step 2: Each input x_i is received and forwarded to higher layers (next hidden).

Step 3: Hidden unit sums its weighted inputs as follows:

$$Z_i = \Sigma x_i w_{ij} + b$$

Where Z_i *is the output with weighted sums,* x_i is the input, w_{ij} are the weights and *b is the bias.*

Step 4: Applying Activation function

$$A_i = f(Z_i)$$

Where A_i *is the Activation Function output, f is the activation function (Sigmoid or Step or Sign). This value is passed to the output layer*

Step 5: Back propagation of Errors

Back propagation Error= Actual Output – Desired Output

Step 6: From the output layer, go back to the hidden layer to adjust the weights to reduce the error.

Step 7: Repeat the process until the desired output is achieved.

Advantages of BPN

- Has smooth effect on weight correction
- Computing time is less if weight's are small
- Faster than perceptron model
- Has a systematic weight updating procedure

Disadvantages of BPN

- Learning phase requires intensive calculations
- Selection of number of Hidden layer neurons is an issue
- Selection of number of Hidden layers is also an issue
- Network gets trapped in Local Minima
- Training time is more for Complex problems

2.4 REGULARIZATION

A fundamental problem in machine learning is how to make an algorithm that will perform well not just on the training data, but also on new inputs. Many strategies used in machine learning are explicitly designed to reduce the test error, possibly at the expense of increased training error. These strategies are known collectively as regularization.

Regularization is a technique that helps reduce overfitting or reduce variance in our network by penalizing for complexity.

In Overfitting, the model tries to learn too many details in the training data along with the noise from the training data. As a result, the model performance is very poor on unseen or test datasets. So over fitting problems can be defined as data performing well in training data and failing or test data.

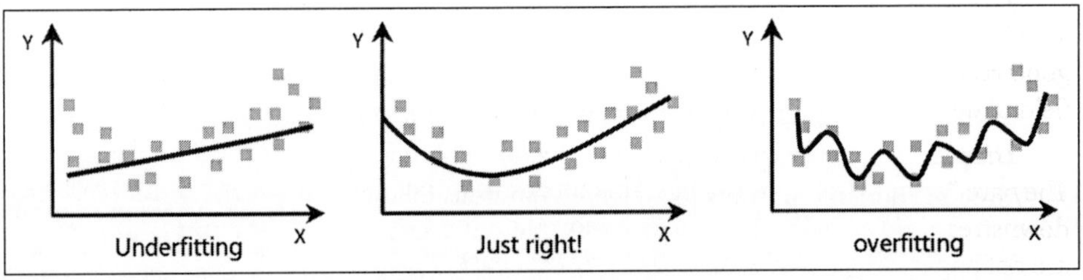

Figure 2.4: *Regularization*

- **Underfit Model**. A model that fails to sufficiently learn the problem and performs poorly on a training dataset and does not perform well on a test sample.
- **Good Fit Model**. A model that suitably learns the training dataset and generalizes well to the test dataset.
- **Overfit Model**. A model that learns the training dataset too well, performing well on the training dataset but does not perform well on a test sample.

Reasons for Overfitting

1. Distribution of weights
2. Number of hidden layers

Different Regularization Techniques

L1 and L2 Regularization

L1 and L2 are the most common types of regularization used to solve overfitting problems caused by distribution of weights. These update the general cost function by adding another term known as the regularization term.

Cost function = Loss (say, binary cross entropy) + Regularization term

Due to the addition of this regularization term, the values of weight matrices decrease because it assumes that a neural network with smaller weight matrices leads to simpler models. Therefore, it will also reduce overfitting to quite an extent.

However, this regularization term differs in L1 and L2.

In L2, we have:

$$Cost\ function = Loss + \frac{\lambda}{2m} \cdot \sum \|w\|^2$$

Here, λ is the regularization parameter. It is the hyperparameter whose value is optimized for better results. L2 regularization is also known as weight decay as it forces the weights to decay towards zero (but not exactly zero).

In L1, we have:

$$Cost\ function = Loss + \frac{\lambda}{2m} * \sum \|\ w\ \|$$

In this, we penalize the absolute value of the weights. Unlike L2, the weights may be reduced to zero here. Hence, it is very useful when we are trying to compress our model. Otherwise, we usually prefer L2 over it.

Dropout

This is one of the most interesting types of regularization techniques. It also produces very good results and is consequently the most frequently used regularization technique in the field of deep learning.

Dropout is a technique where randomly selected neurons are ignored during training. They are "dropped-out" randomly. This means that their contribution to the activation of downstream neurons is temporarily removed on the forward pass and any weight updates are not applied to the neuron on the backward pass.

Dropout may be implemented on any or all hidden layers in the network as well as the visible or input layer. It is not used on the output layer. Dropout regularization is a generic approach.

The default interpretation of the dropout hyperparameter is the probability of training a given node in a layer, where 1.0 means no dropout, and 0.0 means no outputs from the layer. A good value for dropout in a hidden layer is between 0.5 and 0.8. Input layers use a larger dropout rate, such as 0.8.

Dropout is a regularization technique for reducing overfitting in neural networks by preventing complex co-adaptations on training data. It is a very efficient way of performing model averaging with neural networks. The term "dropout" refers to dropping out units (both hidden and visible) in a neural network.

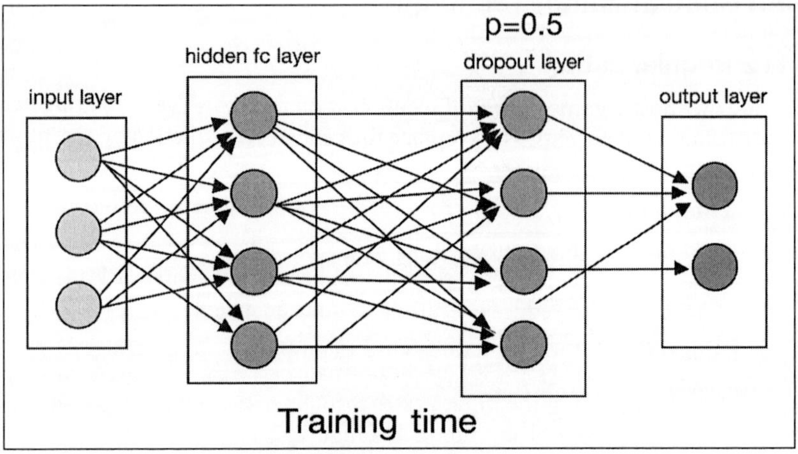

Figure 2.5: *Dropout*

L1 Regularization Vs L2 Regularization

S.No.	L1 Regularization	L2 Regularization
1	Panelizes the sum of absolute value of weights.	Penalizes the sum of square weights.
2	It has a sparse solution.	It has a non-sparse solution.
3	It gives multiple solutions.	It has only one solution.
4	Constructed in feature selection.	No feature selection.
5	Robust to outliers.	Not robust to outliers.
6	It generates simple and interpretable models.	It gives more accurate predictions when the output variable is the function of whole input variables.
7	Unable to learn complex data patterns.	Able to learn complex data patterns.
8	Computationally inefficient over non-parse conditions.	Computationally efficient because of having analytical solutions.

2.5 BATCH NORMALIZATION

It is a method of adaptive reparameterization, motivated by the difficulty of training very deep models. In Deep networks, the weights are updated for each layer. So, the output will no longer be on the same scale as the input (even though input is normalized).

Normalization is a data pre-processing tool used to bring the numerical data to a common scale without distorting its shape. When we input the data to a machine or deep learning algorithm, we tend to change the values to a balanced scale because we ensure that our model can generalize appropriately.

A typical neural network is trained using a collected set of input data called **batch**. Similarly, the normalizing process in batch normalization takes place in batches, not as a single input.

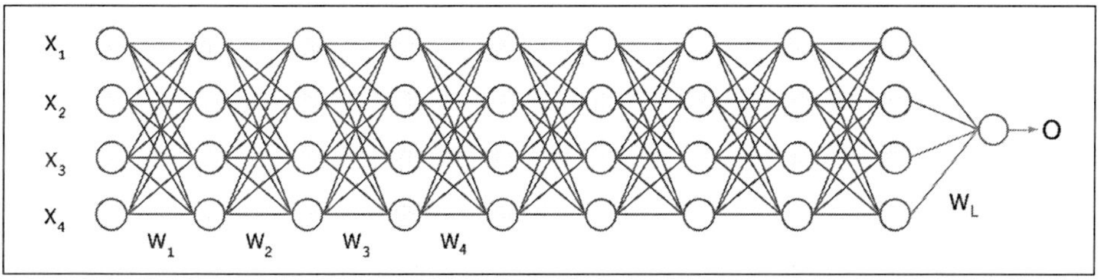

Figure 2.6: *Batch Normalization*

L = Number of layers Bias=0

Activation Function: Sigmoid

Initially, the inputs X1, X2, X3, X4 are in normalized form as they are coming from the pre-processing stage. When the input passes through the first layer, it transforms, as a sigmoid function applied over the dot product of input X and the weight matrix W

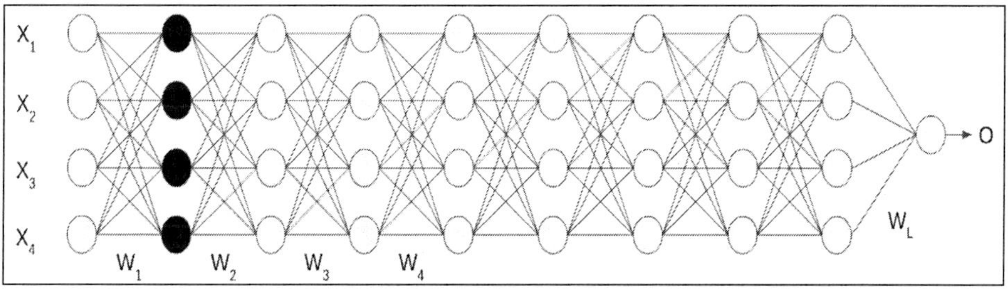

$$h_1 = \sigma(W_1X)$$

Figure 2.6a: *Batch Normalization in Layer 1*

Similarly, this transformation will take place for the second layer and go till the last layer L as shown in the following image.

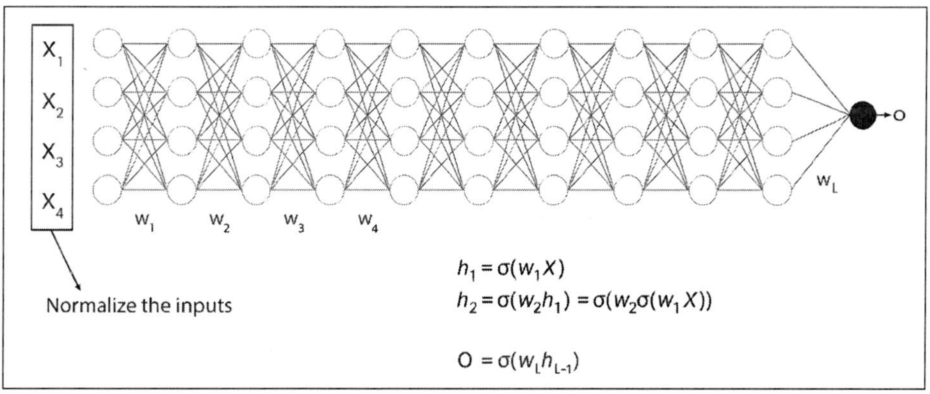

Figure 2.6b: *Batch Normalization in Layer L*

Although our input X was normalized with time the output will no longer be on the same scale. As the data go through multiple layers of the neural network and L activation functions are applied, it leads to an internal covariate shift in the data.

Batch Normalization is a two-step process. First, the input is normalized, and later rescaling and offsetting is performed.

Normalization is the process of transforming the data to have a mean zero and standard deviation one. In this step we have our batch input from layer h, first, we need to calculate the mean of this hidden activation.

$$\mu = \frac{1}{m}\sum h_i$$

Here, m is the number of neurons at layer h. Once we have meant at our end, the next step is to calculate the standard deviation of the hidden activations.

$$\sigma = \left[\frac{1}{m}\Sigma(h_i - \mu)^2\right]^{1/2}$$

Further, as we have the mean and the standard deviation ready. We will normalize the hidden activities using these values. For this, we will subtract the mean from each input and divide the whole value with the sum of standard deviation and the smoothing term (ε).

The smoothing term(ε) assures numerical stability within the operation by stopping a division by a zero value.

$$h_{i(norm)} = \frac{(h_i - \mu)}{\sigma + \varepsilon}$$

Rescaling of Offsetting: In the final operation, the re-scaling and offsetting of the input take place. Here two components of the BN algorithm come into the picture, γ(gamma) and β (beta). These parameters are used for re-scaling (γ) and shifting(β) of the vector containing values from the previous operations.

$$h_i + y\, h_{i(norm)} + \beta$$

These two are learnable parameters, during the training neural network ensures the optimal values of γ and β are used. That will enable the accurate normalization of each batch

Advantages of Batch Normalization

- Speed Up the Training
- Handles internal covariate shift

2.6 VC DIMENSION

The Vapnik-Chervonenkis dimension, more commonly known as the VC dimension, is a model capacity measurement used in statistics and machine learning. It is termed informally as a measure of a model's capacity. It is used frequently to guide the model selection process while developing machine learning applications.The **Vapnik–Chervonenkis (VC) dimension** is a measure of the capacity (complexity, expressive power, richness, or flexibility) of a set of functions that can be learned by a statistical binary classification algorithm.

- It is defined as the cardinality of the largest set of points that the algorithm can shatter.
- It was originally defined by Vladimir Vapnik and Alexey Chervonenkis.

Example

The VC dimension for a linear classifier is *at least* 3, since it can shatter this configuration of 3 points.

In each of the $2^3 = 8$ possible assignments of positive and negative, the classifier is able to perfectly separate the two classes.

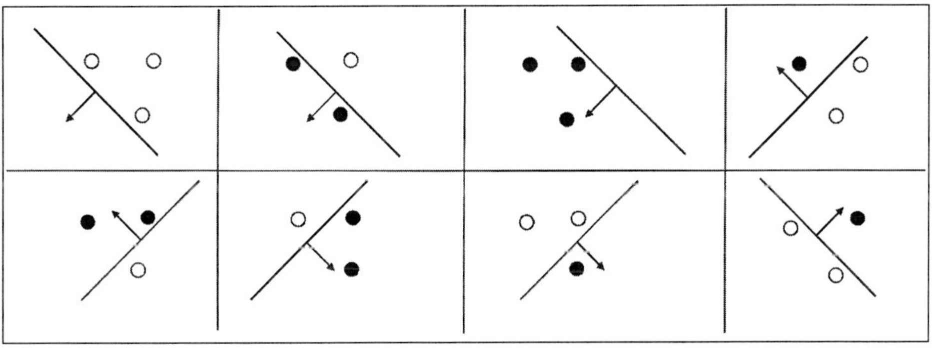

Figure 2.7: *VC dimension for a linear classifier*

VC dimension can also have defined in the form of **set shattering.**

A subset S of instances of a set X is shattered by a collection of function F if

S' ⊆ S there is a function f ∈ F such data:

$$f(x) = \begin{Bmatrix} 1 & \varepsilon \in S' \\ 0 & x \in S - S' \end{Bmatrix}$$

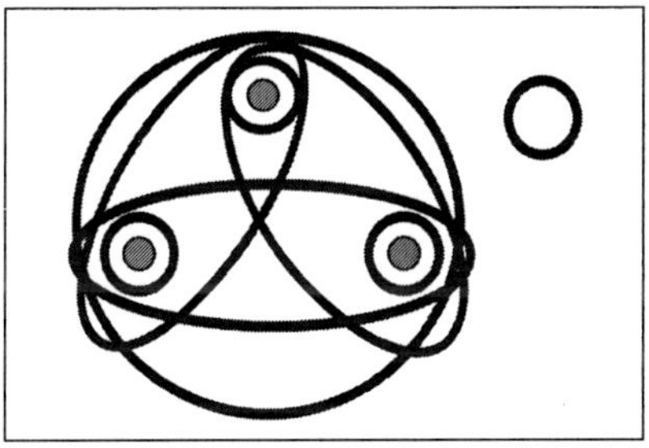

Figure 2.8: *VC Dimension – Set Shattering*

2.7 SHALLOW VS DEEP NETWORK

Sl.No.	Shallow Net's	Deep Learning Net's
1	One Hidden layer (or very less no. of Hidden Layers)	Deep Net's has many layers of Hidden layers with more no. of neurons in each layers
2	Takes input only as VECTORS	DL can have raw data like image, text as inputs
3	Shallow net's needs more parameters to have better fit	DL can fit functions better with less parameters than a shallow network
4	Shallow networks with one Hidden layer (same no of neurons as DL) cannot place complex functions over the input space	DL can compactly express highly complex functions over input space

Sl.No.	Shallow Net's	Deep Learning Net's
5	The number of units in a shallow network grows exponentially with task complexity.	DL don't need to increase it size(neurons) for complex problems
6	Shallow network is more difficult to train with our current algorithms (e.g. it has issues of local minima etc)	Training in DL is easy and no issue of local minima in DL

2.8 CONVOLUTIONAL NEURAL NETWORK

A **Convolutional neural network (CNN)** is a neural network that has one or more convolutional layers and is used mainly for image processing, classification, and segmentation.

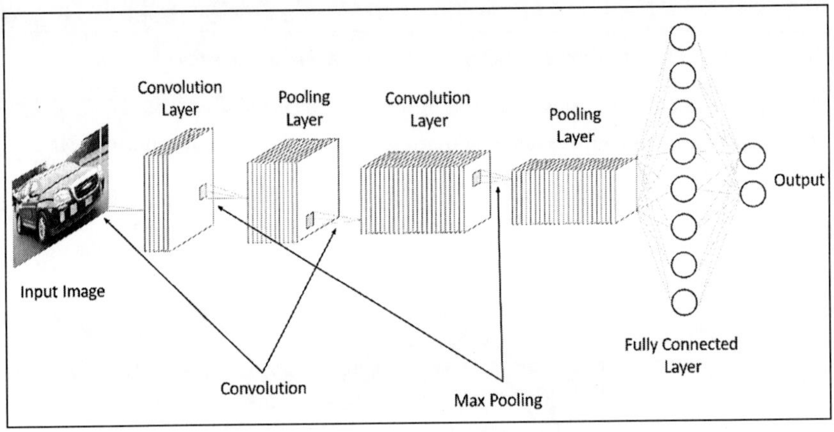

Figure 2.9: *Convolutional Neural Network*

Input layer

The input to a CNN, is mostly an image (nxmx1-gray scale image and nxmx3-colored image)

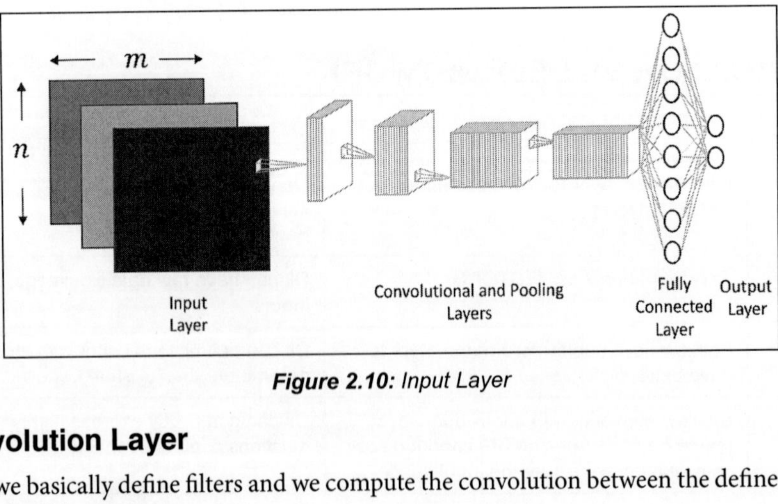

Figure 2.10: *Input Layer*

Convolution Layer

Here, we basically define filters and we compute the convolution between the defined filters and each of the 3 images.

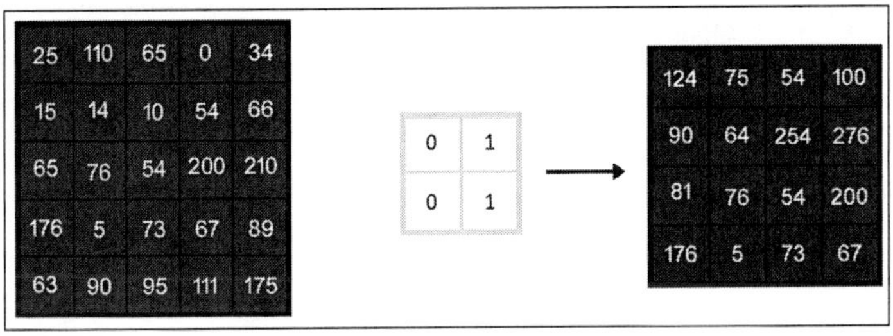

Figure 2.11: *Convolution Layer*

In the same way we apply the remaining (above is for the red image, then we do the same for the green and blue) images. We can apply more than one filter. More filters we use, the better we can preserve spatial dimensions. We use convolution instead of considering flatten images as input as we will end up with a massive number of parameters that will need to be optimized and computationally expensive.

It is worth having the ReLU activation function in the convolution layer which passes only positive values and negative values to zeros.

Pooling layer

Pooling layer objective is to reduce the spatial dimensions of the data propagating through the network.

1. **Max Pooling** is the most common, for each section of the image we scan and keep the highest value.

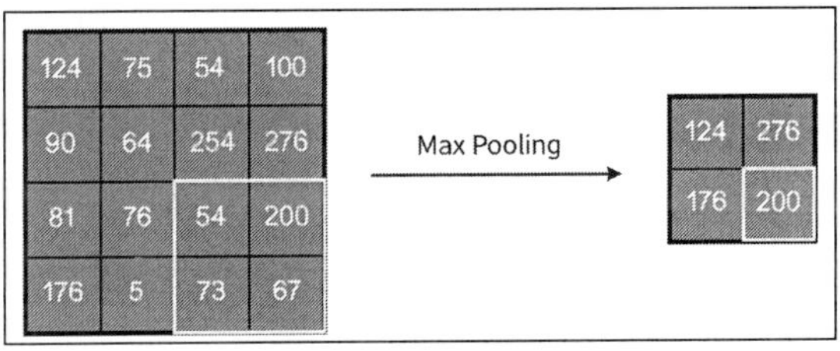

Max Pooling with stride = 2

Figure 2.12: *Max Pooling*

Max pooling provides spatial variance which enables the neural network to recognize objects in an image even if the object does not exactly resemble the original object.

2. **Average Pooling:** Here, we take the average of the area we scan.

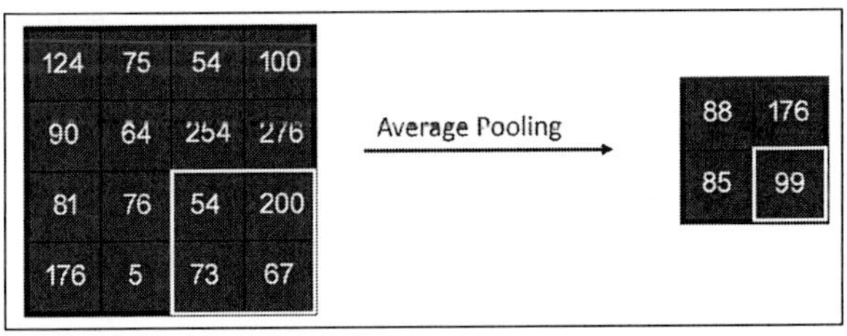

Average Pooling with stride = 2

Figure 2.13: *Average Pooling*

Fully Connected Layer

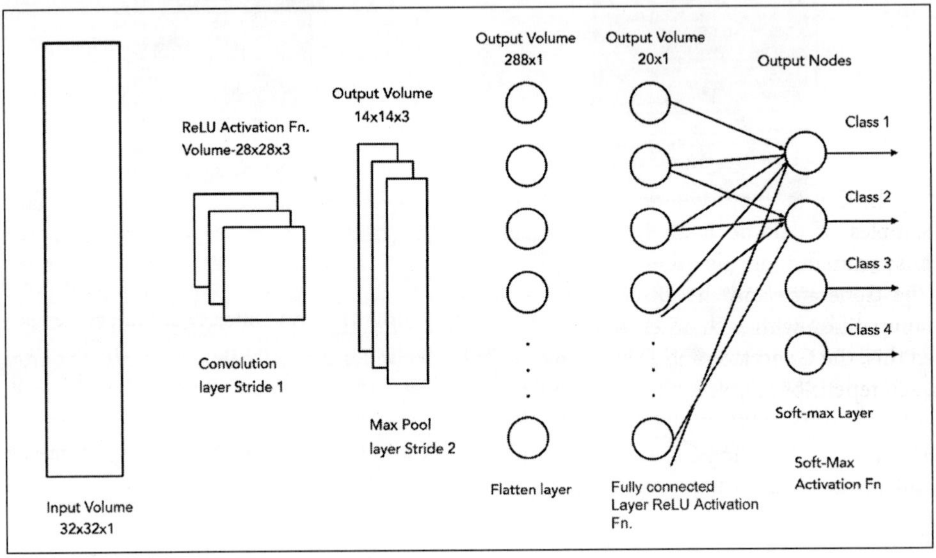

Figure 2.14: *Fully Connected Layer*

Here, we flatten the output of the last convolutional layer and connect every node of the current layer with every other node of the next layer.

Adding a Fully-Connected layer is a (usually) cheap way of learning non-linear combinations of the high-level features as represented by the output of the convolutional layer. The Fully-Connected layer is learning a possibly non-linear function in that space.

Convert input image into a suitable form for our Multi-Level Perceptron, flatten the image into a column vector. The flattened output is fed to a feed-forward neural network and backpropagation applied to every iteration of training. Over a series of epochs, the model is able to distinguish between dominating and certain low-level features in images and classify them using the **Softmax Classification** technique.

There are various architectures of CNNs as,

1. LeNet
2. AlexNet
3. VGGNet
4. GoogLeNet
5. ResNet
6. ZFNet

2.9 GENERATIVE ADVERSARIAL NETWORKS (GANS)

Generative Adversarial Networks (GANs) are a powerful class of neural networks that are used for unsupervised learning. It was developed and introduced by Ian J. Goodfellow in 2014. GANs are basically made up of a system of two competing neural network models which compete with each other and are able to analyze, capture and copy the variations within a dataset.

Generative Adversarial Networks (GANs) can be broken down into three parts:

- **Generative:** To learn a generative model, which describes how data is generated in terms of a probabilistic model.
- **Adversarial:** The training of a model is done in an adversarial setting.
- **Networks:** Use deep neural networks as the artificial intelligence (AI) algorithms for training purposes.

In GANs, there is a **generator** and a **discriminator**. The Generator generates fake samples of data(be it an image, audio, etc.) and tries to fool the Discriminator. The Discriminator, on the other hand, tries to distinguish between the real and fake samples. The Generator and the Discriminator are both Neural Networks and they both run in competition with each other in the training phase. The steps are repeated several times and in this, the Generator and Discriminator get better and better in their respective jobs after each repetition.

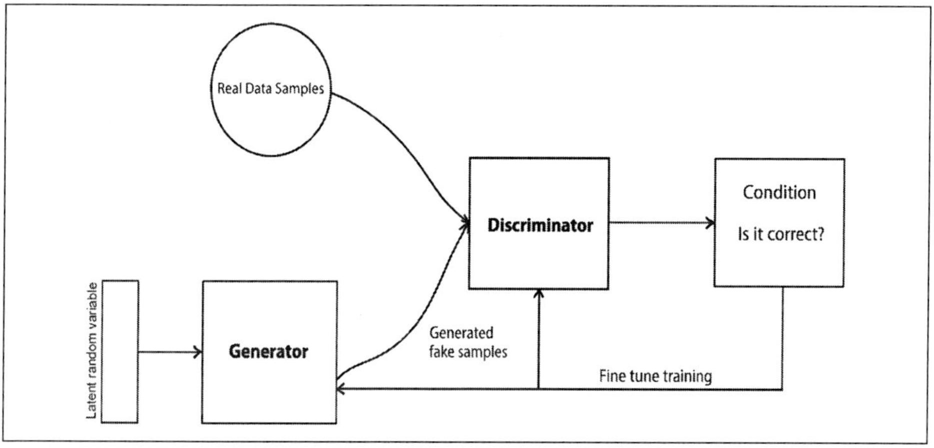

***Figure 2.15:** Generative Adversarial Networks*

Here, the generative model captures the distribution of data and is trained in such a manner that it tries to maximize the probability of the Discriminator in making a mistake. The Discriminator, on the other hand, is based on a model that estimates the probability that the sample that it got is received from the training data and not from the Generator.

The GANs are formulated as a minimax game, where the Discriminator is trying to minimize its reward **V(D, G)** and the Generator is trying to minimize the Discriminator's reward or in other words, maximize its loss. It can be mathematically described by the formula below:

$$\min_{G} \max_{D} V(D, G)$$

$$V(D, G) = E_{x \sim pdata(x)}[\log D(x)] + E_{z \sim p_z(z)}[\log(1 - D)(G(z))]$$

where,

- G = Generator
- D = Discriminator
- Pdata(x) = distribution of real data
- P(z) = distribution of generator

- x = sample from Pdata(x)
- z = sample from P(z)
- D(x) = Discriminator network
- G(z) = Generator network

So, basically, training a GAN has two parts:

- **Part 1:** The Discriminator is trained while the Generator is idle. In this phase, the network is only forward propagated and no back-propagation is done. The Discriminator is trained on real data for n epochs, and sees if it can correctly predict them as real. Also, in this phase, the Discriminator is also trained on the fake generated data from the Generator and see if it can correctly predict them as fake.
- **Part 2:** The Generator is trained while the Discriminator is idle. After the Discriminator is trained by the generated fake data of the Generator, we can get its predictions and use the results for training the Generator and get better from the previous state to try and fool the Discriminator.

The above method is repeated for a few epochs and then manually checks the fake data if it seems genuine. If it seems acceptable, then the training is stopped, otherwise, it's allowed to continue for a few more epochs.

Different Types of GANs

1. **Vanilla GAN:** This is the simplest type of GAN. Here, the Generator and the Discriminator are simple multi-layer perceptrons. In vanilla GAN, the algorithm is really simple, it tries to optimize the mathematical equation using stochastic gradient descent.
2. **Conditional GAN (CGAN):** CGAN can be described as a deep learning method in which some conditional parameters are put into place. In CHAN, an additional parameter 'y' is added to the Generator for generating the corresponding data.
3. **Deep Convolutional GAN (DCGAN):** DCGAN is one of the most popular and also the most successful implementations of GAN. It is composed of ConvNets in place of multi-layer perceptrons.
4. **Laplacian Pyramid GAN (LAPGAN):** The Laplacian pyramid is a linear invertible image representation consisting of a set of band-pass images, spaced an octave apart, plus a low-frequency residual.
5. **Super Resolution GAN (SRGAN):** SRGAN as the name suggests is a way of designing a GAN in which a deep neural network is used along with an adversarial network in order to produce higher resolution images. This type of GAN is particularly useful in optimally up-scaling native low-resolution images to enhance its details, minimizing errors while doing so.

2.10 SEMI-SUPERVISED LEARNING

Semi-supervised learning (SSL) is a machine learning technique that uses a small portion of labeled data and lots of unlabeled data to train a predictive model.

Supervised learning is training a machine learning model using the labeled dataset. Organic labels are often available in data, but the process may involve a human expert that adds tags to raw data to show a model the target attributes (answers). In simple terms, a label is basically a description showing a model what it is expected to predict.

Supervised learning has a few limitations as,

- *slow* (it requires human experts to manually label training examples one by one) and
- *costly* (a model should be trained on the large volumes of hand-labeled data to provide accurate predictions).

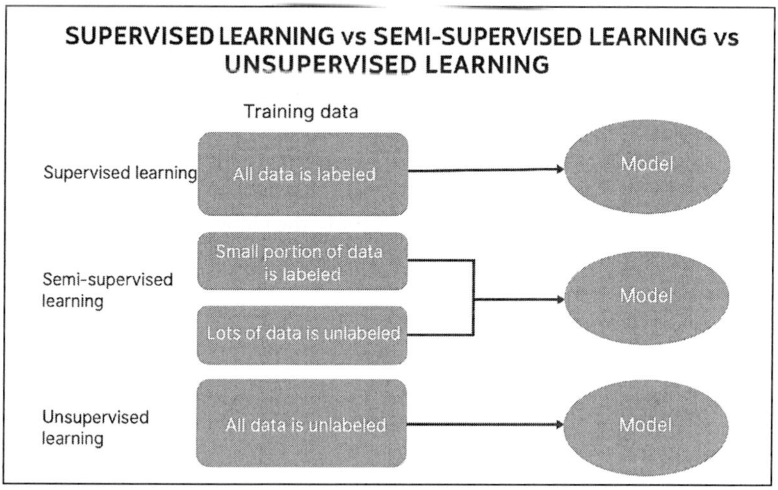

Figure 2.16: *Semi-Supervised Learning*

Unsupervised learning, on the other hand, is when a model tries to mine hidden patterns, differences, and similarities in unlabeled data by itself, without human supervision. Hence the name. Within this method, data points are grouped into clusters based on similarities.

While unsupervised learning is a cheaper way to perform training tasks, it isn't a silver bullet. Commonly it is,

- has a *limited area of applications* (mostly for clustering purposes) and
- provides *less accurate results.*
- **Semi-supervised learning** bridges supervised learning and unsupervised learning techniques to solve their key challenges. With it, you train an initial model on a few labeled samples and then iteratively apply it to the greater number of unlabeled data.
  - Unlike unsupervised learning, SSL works for a variety of problems from classification and regression to clustering and association.
  - Unlike supervised learning, the method uses small amounts of labeled data and also large amounts of unlabeled data, which reduces expenses on manual annotation and cuts data preparation time.

Assumptions followed by Semi-Supervised Learning

To work with the unlabeled dataset, there must be a relationship between the objects. To understand this, semi-supervised learning uses any of the following assumptions:

- **Continuity Assumption:** As per the continuity assumption, the objects near each other tend to share the same group or label. This assumption is also used in supervised learning, and the datasets are separated by the decision boundaries. But in semi-supervised, the decision boundaries are added with the smoothness assumption in low-density boundaries.
- **Cluster assumptions**- In this assumption, data are divided into different discrete clusters. Further, the points in the same cluster share the output label.
- **Manifold assumptions**- This assumption helps to use distances and densities, and this data lie on a manifold of fewer dimensions than input space.
- The dimensional data are created by a process that has less degree of freedom and may be hard to model directly. **(This assumption becomes practical if high).**

Working of Semi-Supervised Learning

Semi-supervised learning uses pseudo labeling to train the model with less labeled training data than supervised learning. The process can combine various neural network models and training ways.

- Firstly, it trains the model with less amount of training data similar to the supervised learning models. The training continues until the model gives accurate results.
- The algorithms use the unlabeled dataset with pseudo labels in the next step, and now the result may not be accurate. Now, the labels from labeled training data and pseudo labels data are linked together.
- The input data in labeled training data and unlabeled training data are also linked.
- In the end, again train the model with the new combined input as did in the first step. It will reduce errors and improve the accuracy of the model.

Semi-supervised Learning Models Applications

- Speech Analysis
- Web content classification
- Protein sequence classification
- Text document classifier

UNIT 3

Dimensionality Reduction

3.1 COMPONENTS OF DIMENSIONALITY REDUCTION

There are two components of dimensionality reduction:

1. **Feature selection:** In this, we try to find a subset of the original set of variables, or features, to get a smaller subset which can be used to model the problem. It usually involves three ways:
   - Filter
   - Wrapper
   - Embedded
2. **Feature extraction:** This reduces the data in a high dimensional space to a lower dimension space, i.e. a space with lesser no. of dimensions.

Methods of Dimensionality Reduction

The various methods used for dimensionality reduction include:

- Principal Component Analysis (PCA)
- Linear Discriminant Analysis (LDA)
- Generalized Discriminant Analysis (GDA)

Advantages of Dimensionality Reduction

- It helps in data compression, and hence reduced storage space.
- It reduces computation time.
- It also helps remove redundant features, if any.

Disadvantages of Dimensionality Reduction

- It may lead to some amount of data loss.
- PCA tends to find linear correlations between variables, which is sometimes undesirable.
- PCA fails in cases where mean and covariance are not enough to define datasets.

3.2 PRINCIPAL COMPONENT ANALYSIS (PCA)

This method was introduced by Karl Pearson. It works on a condition that while the data in a higher dimensional space is mapped to data in a lower dimension space, the variance of the data in the lower dimensional space should be maximum.

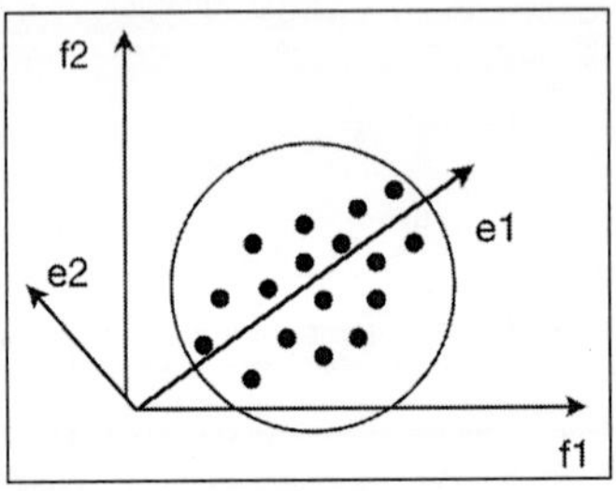

Figure 3.1: *Principal Component Analysis*

It involves the following steps:

- Construct the covariance matrix of the data.
- Compute the eigenvectors of this matrix.
- Eigenvectors corresponding to the largest eigenvalues are used to reconstruct a large fraction of variance of the original data.

Hence, we are left with a lesser number of eigenvectors, and there might have been some data loss in the process. But, the most important variances should be retained by the remaining eigenvectors.

Principal Component Analysis (PCA)

Reduce the given set of features to 1

x	4	8	13	7
y	11	4	5	14

Step-1: No of features $n = 2$

Samples $N = 4$

Step-2: Mean of x,

$$\bar{x} = \frac{4+8+13+7}{4} = \frac{32}{4} = 8$$

$$\bar{y} = \frac{11+4+5+14}{4} = \frac{20+14}{4} = \frac{34}{4} = 8.5$$

$$(\bar{x}, \bar{y}) = (8,8.5)$$

Step 3: Computation of covariance matrix ordered pairs are :

Covariance of all ordered pairs

$(x, x), (x, y)(y, x), (y, y)$

$$(\text{Cov}(x, x) = \frac{1}{N\boxtimes 1}\sum_{k\boxtimes=1}^{N} (x_{ik} - \bar{x}_i)(x_{ik} - \bar{x}_i)$$

$$= \frac{1}{4\boxtimes 1}\left[(4-8)^2 + (8-8)^2 + (13-8)^2 + (7-8)^2\right]$$

$$\text{Cov}(x,y) = \frac{1}{4\boxtimes 1}[(4-8)(11-8.5) + (8-8)(4-8.5) + (13-8)(5-8.5) + (7-8)$$
$$(14-8-5)] = -11$$

$\mathrm{Cov}(y, x) = -11$

$$\mathrm{Cov}(y,y) = \frac{1}{4⊠1}\,[(11 - 8.5)^2 + (4 - 8.5)^2 + (5 - 8.5)^2 + (14 - 8.5)^2] = 23$$

Covariance matrix is given by

$$S = \begin{bmatrix} \mathrm{Cov}(x,x) & \mathrm{Cov}(x,y) \\ \mathrm{Cov}(y,x) & \mathrm{Cov}(y,y) \end{bmatrix}$$

$$S = \begin{bmatrix} 14 & -11 \\ -11 & 23 \end{bmatrix}$$

Step 4 : Calculate the Eigen Values

The equation to calculate the eigen value is given by,

$$|S - \lambda I| = 0$$

Where,

S is the covariance matrix

λ is the eigen value

I is the Identity matrix

$$\left|\begin{bmatrix} 14 & -11 \\ -11 & 23 \end{bmatrix} - \lambda \begin{bmatrix} 1 & 0 \\ 0 & 1 \end{bmatrix}\right| = 0$$

$$\left|\begin{bmatrix} 14-\lambda & -11 \\ -11 & 23-\lambda \end{bmatrix}\right| = 0$$

$$(14-\lambda)(23-\lambda)-(-11)(23-\lambda)=0$$

$$\lambda^2 - 37\lambda + 201 = 0$$

Solving the quadratic equation , we get

$\lambda_1 = 30.3849$, $\lambda_2 = 6.6151$

Here $\lambda_1 > \lambda_2$

λ_1 gives the principal component.

Calculate the eigen vector for λ_1

$(S - \lambda_1 I)U_1 = 0$

$$\begin{bmatrix} 14-\lambda & -11 \\ -11 & 23-\lambda_1 \end{bmatrix}\begin{bmatrix} u_1 \\ U_2 \end{bmatrix} = 0$$

$$\begin{bmatrix} (14-\lambda_1)\mathrm{u}_1 - 11\mathrm{u}_2 \\ -11\mathrm{u}_1 + (23-\lambda 1)u_2 \end{bmatrix} = \begin{bmatrix} 0 \\ 0 \end{bmatrix}$$

$$(14-\lambda_1)u_1 - 11u_2 = 0$$

$$-11u_1 + (23-\lambda)u_2 = 0$$

$$\frac{u_1}{11} = \frac{u^2}{14-\lambda_1} = 1$$

$$\frac{1}{\sqrt{u_1^2+u_1^2}}\begin{bmatrix} u_2 \\ u_2 \end{bmatrix}$$

When $u_1 = 11$

$u_2 = 14 - \lambda_1$

Eigen vector U1 of $\lambda_1 = \begin{bmatrix} 11 \\ 14-\lambda_1 \end{bmatrix} = \begin{bmatrix} 11 \\ 14-30.38 \end{bmatrix} = \begin{vmatrix} 11 \\ -16.38 \end{vmatrix}$

Normalize the eigen vector U1

$$el = \frac{1}{\sqrt{u_1^2+u_1^2}}\begin{bmatrix} u_2 \\ u_2 \end{bmatrix}$$

$$= \frac{1}{\sqrt{11^2+(-16.38)^2}}\begin{bmatrix} 11 \\ -16.38 \end{bmatrix}$$

The eigen vector U1 of

$$e2 = \begin{bmatrix} 0.8303 \\ 0.5574 \end{bmatrix}$$

Step 5 : Derive the new dataset

Data samples	Ex1	Ex2	Ex3	Ex3
First Principal Component PC1	P11	P12	P13	P14

$$P11 = e1^T\begin{bmatrix} x1-\bar{x} \\ y1-\bar{y} \end{bmatrix}$$

$$= [0.5574\ -0.8303]\begin{bmatrix} 4-8 \\ 11-8.5 \end{bmatrix}$$

$$= [0.5574\ -0.8303]\begin{bmatrix} 4-8 \\ 11-8.5 \end{bmatrix}$$

$$= [0.5574\ -0.8303]\begin{bmatrix} -4 \\ 2.5 \end{bmatrix}$$

$$= -4.3052$$

$$P12 = e1^T\begin{bmatrix} x2-\bar{x} \\ y2-\bar{y} \end{bmatrix}$$

$$= [0.5574 - 0.8303]\begin{bmatrix} 8-8 \\ 4-8.5 \end{bmatrix}$$

$$=3.7361$$

$$P13 \;= e1^{T}\begin{bmatrix} x3-\bar{x} \\ y3-\bar{y} \end{bmatrix}$$

$$= [5.5574\ -0.8303]\begin{bmatrix} 13-8 \\ 5-8.5 \end{bmatrix}$$

$$= 5.6928$$

$$P14 \;= e1^{T}\begin{bmatrix} x4-\bar{x} \\ y4-y \end{bmatrix}$$

$$= [5.5574\ -0.8303]\begin{bmatrix} 7-8 \\ 14-8.5 \end{bmatrix}$$

$$= -5.1288$$

Data samples	Ex1	Ex2	Ex3	Ex3
First Principal Component PC1	-4.3052	3.7361	5.6928	-5.1238

3.3 LINEAR DISCRIMINANT ANALYSIS (LDA)

Linear Discriminant Analysis (LDA) is one of the commonly used dimensionality reduction techniques in machine learning to solve more than two-class classification problems. It is also known as Normal Discriminant Analysis (NDA) or Discriminant Function Analysis (DFA).

Linear Discriminant analysis is one of the most popular dimensionality reduction techniques used for supervised classification problems in machine learning. *It is also considered a pre-processing step for modeling differences in ML and applications of pattern classification.*

Extension to Linear Discriminant Analysis (LDA)

Linear Discriminant analysis is one of the most simple and effective methods to solve classification problems in machine learning. It has so many extensions and variations as follows:

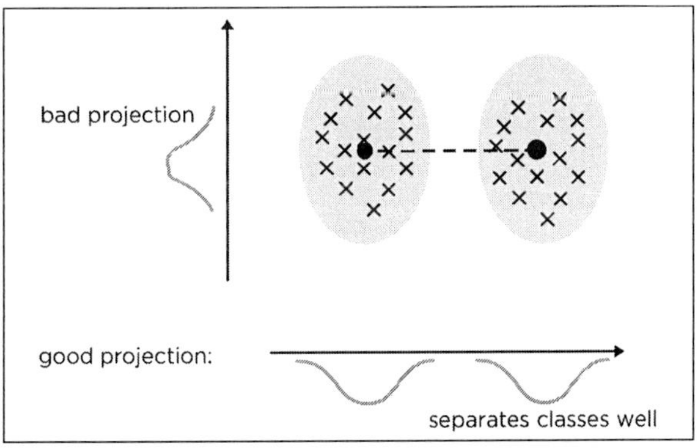

Figure 3.2: *Linear Discriminant Analysis*

1. **Quadratic Discriminant Analysis (QDA):** For multiple input variables, each class deploys its own estimate of variance.
2. **Flexible Discriminant Analysis (FDA):** it is used when non-linear groups of inputs are used, such as splines.
3. **Flexible Discriminant Analysis (FDA):** This uses regularization in the estimate of the variance (actually covariance) and hence moderates the influence of different variables on LDA.

LDA is a type of Linear combination, a mathematical process using various data items and applying a function to that site to separately analyze multiple classes of objects or items. Fisher's Linear discriminant, linear discriminant analysis can be useful in areas like image recognition and predictive analysis in marketing.

LDA Algorithm

First general steps for performing a Linear Discriminant Analysis

1. Compute the d-dimensional mean vector for the different classes from the dataset.
2. Compute the Scatter matrix (in between class and within the class scatter matrix)
3. Sort the EigenVector by decrease Eigenvalue and choose k eigenvector with the largest eigenvalue to from a d x k dimensional matrix w (where every column represent an eigenvector)
4. Used **d * k** eigenvector matrix to transform the sample onto the new subspace.
5. This can be summarized by the matrix multiplication.
6. Y = X x W (where X is a **n * d** dimension matrix representing the n samples and you are transformed **n * k** dimensional samples in the new subspace.

3.4 MANIFOLD LEARNING

It is a popular and quickly-growing subfield of machine learning based on the assumption that one's observed data lie on a low-dimensional manifold embedded in a higher-dimensional space. This thesis presents a mathematical perspective on manifold learning, delving into the intersection of kernel learning, spectral graph theory, and differential geometry. Emphasis is placed on the remarkable interplay between graphs and manifolds, which forms the foundation for the widely-used technique of manifold regularization.

3.5 METRIC LEARNING

A Metric is a non-negative function between two points x and y that describes the distance between two points. Metric learning is an approach on a distance metric that aims to establish similarity or dissimilarity between images. Deep Metric Learning on the other hand uses Neural Networks to automatically learn discriminative features from the images and then compute the metric.

Properties that a metric must satisfy:

1. Non-negativity => $d(x,y) \geq 0$ and $d(x,y) = 0$, if $x = y$
2. Triangular inequality => $d(x,y)$ $d(x,z) + d(z,y)$
3. Symmetry => $g(x,y) = g(y,x)$

Types of Metrics

1. The Euclidean Metric

$$d(x, y) = \sqrt{\sum_{I=1}^{d} (x_i - y_i)^2}$$

In a 'd' dimensional vector space, the metric between 2 points x and y is:

2. The Discrete Metric:

The metric between 2 points x and y is given by:

$$d(x, y) = \begin{cases} 1 & \text{if } x \neq y \\ 1 & \text{if } x = y \end{cases}$$

Mahalanobis Distance Metric:

The metric between 2 matrices x and y is given by:

$$d(x, y) = ((x - y)^T M (x - y))2$$

Where T is the transform matrix and M is the inverse of the covariance matrix.

3.6 AUTO ENCODERS AND DIMENSIONALITY REDUCTION IN NETWORKS

Autoencoder is an unsupervised artificial neural network that compresses the data to a lower dimension and then reconstructs the input back. Autoencoder finds the representation of the data in a lower dimension by focusing more on the important features, getting rid of noise and redundancy. It's based on Encoder- Decoder architecture, where encoder encodes the high-dimensional data to lower-dimension and decoder takes the lower-dimensional data and tries to reconstruct the original high-dimensional data.

AutoEncoder attempts to encode the data by compressing it into the lower dimensions (bottleneck layer or code) and then decoding the data to reconstruct the original input. The bottleneck layer (or code) holds the compressed representation of the input data.

Autoencoders are a specific type of feed forward neural networks where the input is the same as the output. They compress the input into a lower- dimensional code and then reconstruct the output from this representation. The code is a compact "summary" or "compression" of the input, also called the latent-space representation.

An autoencoder consists of 3 components: encoder, code and decoder. The encoder compresses the input and produces the code, the decoder then reconstructs the input only using this code.

Autoencoders are mainly a dimensionality reduction (or compression) algorithm with a couple of important properties:

- **Data-specific**: Autoencoders are only able to meaningfully compress data similar to what they have been trained on. So we can't expect an autoencoder trained on handwritten digits to compress landscape photos.
- **Lossy:** The output of the autoencoder will not be exactly the same as the input, it will be a close but degraded representation.

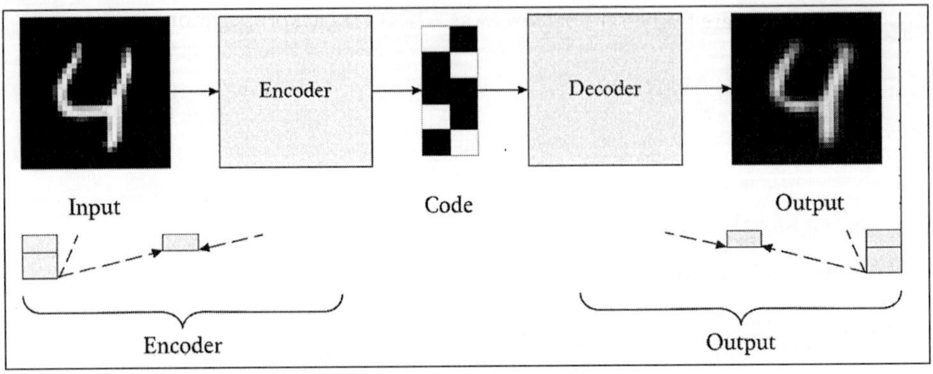

Figure 3.3: *Artificial Neural Network*

- **Unsupervised:** To train an autoencoder we don't need to do anything fancy, just throw the raw input data at it. Autoencoders are considered an *unsupervised* learning technique since they don't need explicit labels to train on. But to be more precise they are *self-supervised* because they generate their own labels from the training data.

First the input passes through the encoder, which is a fully-connected ANN, to produce the code. The decoder, which has the similar ANN structure, then produces the output only using the code.

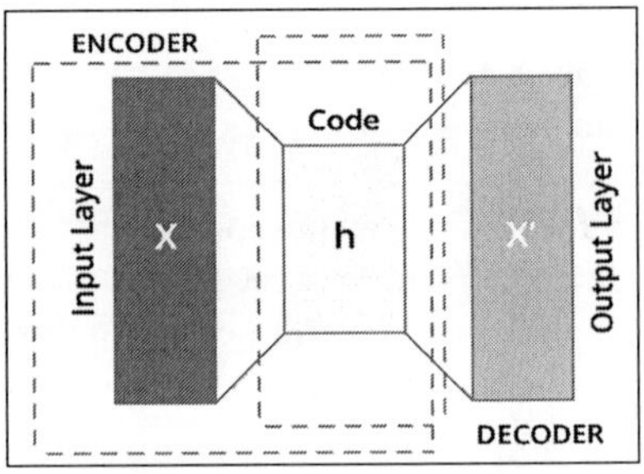

Figure 3.4: *Schema of a basic Autoencoder*

The goal is to get an output identical with the input. The only requirement is the dimensionality of the input and output needs to be the same. Anything in the middle can be played with.

There are 4 hyperparameters that we need to set before training an autoencoder:

- **Code size**: number of nodes in the middle layer. Smaller size results in more compression.
- **Number of layers**: the autoencoder can be as deep as we like. In the figure above we have 2 layers in both the encoder and decoder, without considering the input and output.
- **Number of nodes per layer**: the autoencoder architecture we're working on is called a *stacked autoencoder* since the layers are stacked one after another. Usually stacked autoencoders look like a "sandwich". The number of nodes per layer decreases with each subsequent layer of the encoder, and increases back in the decoder.
- **Loss function**: we either use *mean squared error (mse)* or *binary cross entropy.* If the input values are in the range [0, 1] then we typically use cross entropy, otherwise we use the mean squared error.
    - Number of layers in encoder and decoder.
    - Activation function
    - Optimization function

Autoencoders are trained the same way as ANNs via backpropagation.

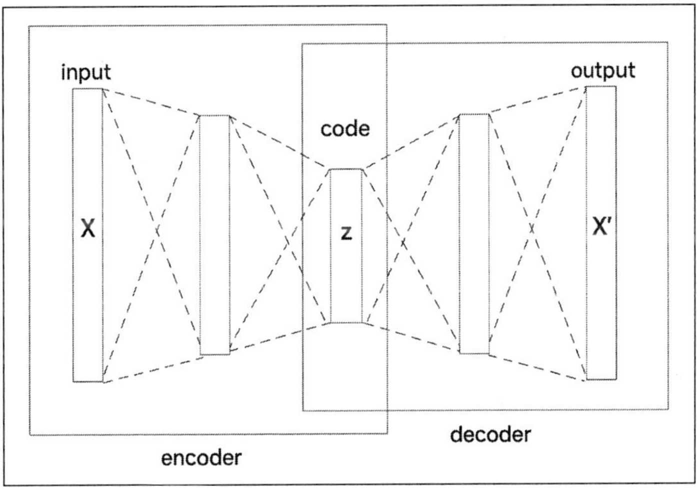

Figure 3.5: *Deep Autoencoder*

In the above Diagram, X is the input data, z is the lower-dimension representation of input X and X' is the reconstructed input data. The mapping of higher to lower dimensions can be linear or non-linear depending on the choice of the activation function.

Types of AutoEncoders

- Deep Autoencoder
- Sparse Autoencoder
- Under complete Autoencoder
- Variational Autoencoder
- LSTM Autoencoder

Applications of AutoEncoders

- Dimensionality reduction
- Anomaly detection
- Image denoising
- Image compression
- Image generation

3.7 INTRODUCTION TO CONVNET

A convolutional neural network (CNN) is a type of artificial neural network used in image recognition and processing that is specifically designed to process pixel data.

CNNs are powerful image processing, artificial intelligence (AI) that use deep learning to perform both generative and descriptive tasks, often using machine vision that includes image and video recognition, along with recommender systems and natural language processing (NLP).

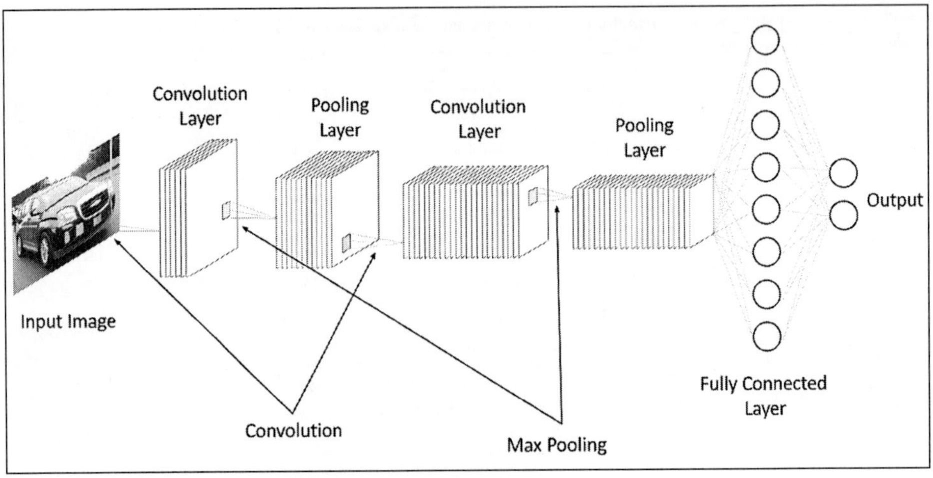

Figure 3.6: *Introduction to Convnet*

3.7.1 AlexNet

Alexnet won the Imagenet large-scale visual recognition challenge in 2012. The model was proposed in 2012 in the research paper named Imagenet Classification with Deep Convolutional Neural Network by Alex Krizhevsky.

The architecture consists of eight layers: five convolutional layers and three fully-connected layers. AlexNet had 60 million parameters, a major issue in terms of overfitting. Two methods were employed to reduce overfitting:

1. Data Augmentation

The authors used label-preserving transformation to make their data more varied. Specifically, they generated image translations and horizontal reflections, which increased the training set by a factor of 2048. They also performed Principle Component Analysis (PCA) on the RGB pixel values to change the intensities of RGB channels, which reduced the top-1 error rate by more than 1%.

2. Dropout

This technique consists of "turning off" neurons with a predetermined probability (e.g. 50%). This means that every iteration uses a different sample of the model's parameters, which forces each neuron to have more robust features that can be used with other random neurons. However, dropout also increases the training time needed for the model's convergence.

- AlexNet was the first convolution Network which used GPU to boost performance.
- AlexNet architecture consists of 5 convolutional layers, 3 max-pooling layers, 2 normalization layers, 2 fully connected layers, and 1 softmax layer.
- Each convolutional layer consists of convolutional filters and a nonlinear activation function ReLU.
- The pooling layers are used to perform max pooling.
- Input size is fixed due to the presence of fully connected layers.

- The input size is mentioned at most of the places as 224x224x3 but due to some padding which happens it works out to be 227x227x3
- AlexNet overall has 60 million parameters.

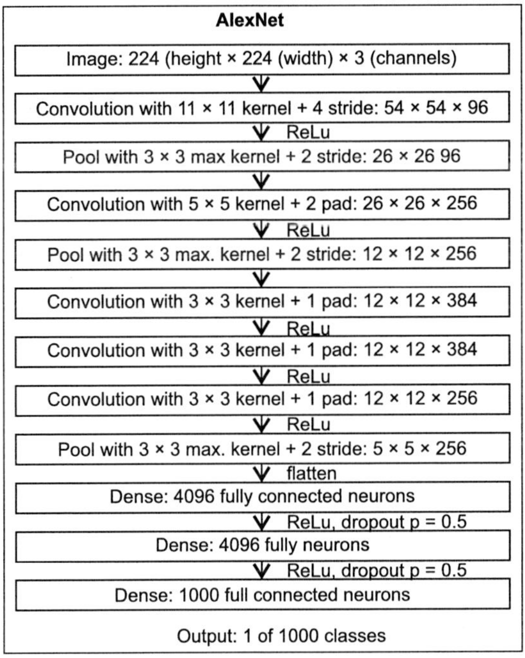

***Figure 3.7:** AlexNet Architecture*

3.7.2 Visual Geometry Group(VGG)

The input to VGG based convNet is a 224*224 RGB image. Preprocessing layer takes the RGB image with pixel values in the range of 0–255 and subtracts the mean image values which is calculated over the entire ImageNet training set. There are a total of 13 convolutional layers and 3 fully connected layers in VGG16. VGG has smaller filters (3*3) with more depth instead of having large filters. It has ended up having the same effective receptive field as if you only have one 7 x 7 convolutional layer.

Another variation of VGGNet has 19 weight layers consisting of 16 convolutional layers with 3 fully connected layers and the same 5 pooling layers. In both variations of VGGNet there consists of two Fully Connected layers with 4096 channels each which is followed by another fully connected layer with 1000 channels to predict 1000 labels. Last fully connected layer uses the softmax layer for classification purposes.

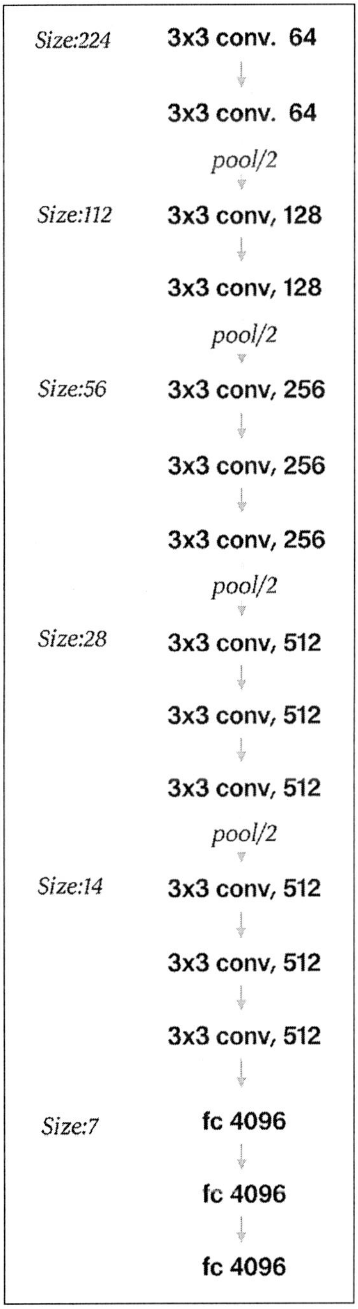

***Figure 3.8**: VGG 16 Architecture*

Limitations of VGG 16

- It is very slow to train (the original VGG model was trained on the Nvidia Titan GPU for 2-3 weeks).
- The size of VGG-16 trained imageNet weights is *528* MB. So, it takes quite a lot of disk space and bandwidth which makes it inefficient.
- 138 million parameters lead to exploding gradients problem.

3.7.3 Inception

Inception Net is a victory over the previous versions of CNN models. It achieves an accuracy of top-5 on ImageNet, it reduces the computational cost to a great extent without compromising the speed and accuracy.

This architecture has *22* layers in total. Using the dimension-reduced inception module, a neural network architecture is constructed. This is popularly known as **GoogLeNet (Inception v1)**. GoogLeNet has *9* such inception modules fitted linearly. It is *22* layers deep (*27*, including the pooling layers). At the end of the architecture, fully connected layers were replaced by a global average pooling which calculates the average of every feature map.

1 X 1 convolution: A *1×1* convolution simply maps an input pixel with all its respective channels to an output pixel. *1×1* convolution is used as a dimensionality reduction module to reduce computation to an extent.

For instance, we need to perform *5×5* convolution without using *1×1* convolution as below:

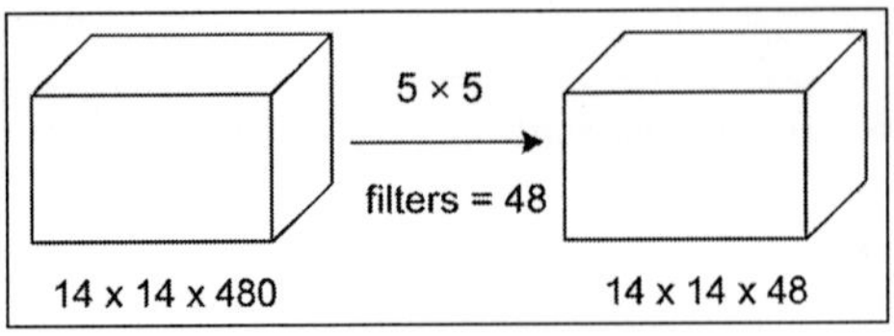

Figure 3.9: *5x5 convolution*

Number of operations involved here is $(14\times14\times48) \times (5\times5\times480) = 112.9M$

Using 1×1 convolution:

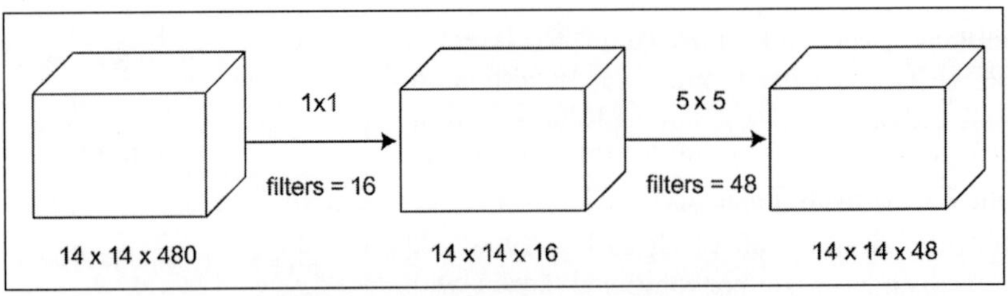

Figure 3.10: *Inducing 1x1 convolution*

Number of operations for 1 × 1 convolution = $(14 \times 14 \times 16) \times (1 \times 1 \times 480) = 1.5M$

Number of operations for 5 × 5 convolution = $(14 \times 14 \times 48) \times (5 \times 5 \times 16) = 3.8M$

After addition we get, $1.5M + 3.8M = 5.3M$

Thus, 1×1 convolution can help to reduce model size which can also somehow help to reduce the overfitting problem.

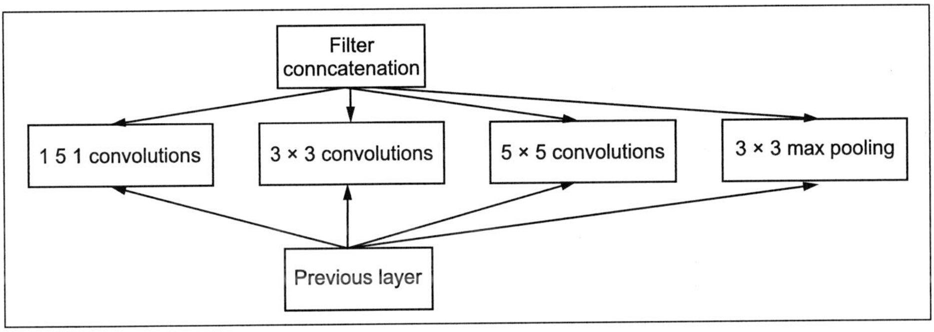

Figure 3.11: *Inception Architecture*

The above depicted Inception module simultaneously performs 1 * 1 convolutions, 3 * 3 convolutions, 5 * 5 convolutions, and 3 * 3 max pooling operations. Thereafter, it sums up the outputs from all the operations in a single place and builds the next feature. The architecture does not follow a Sequential model approach where every operation such as pooling or convolution is performed one after the other.

Disadvantages: Larger model models using Inception Net are prone to over fit especially with limited number of label samples. The model can be biased towards certain classes that have labels present in higher volume than the other.

3.7.4 Residual Network

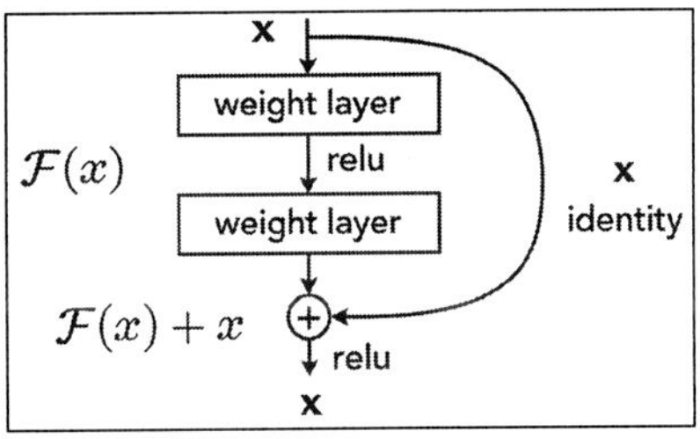

Figure 3.12: *Skip Connections*

In order to solve the problem of the vanishing/exploding gradient, this architecture introduced the concept called Residual Blocks. In this network, we use a technique called ***skip connections***.

The skip connection connects activations of a layer to further layers by skipping some layers in between. This forms a residual block. Resnets are made by stacking these residual blocks together. The approach behind this network is instead of layers learning the underlying mapping, we allow the network to fit the residual mapping. So, instead of say H(x), initial mapping, let the network fit, ***F(x) := H(x) - x* which gives *H(x) := F(x) + x***

The advantage of adding this type of skip connection is that if any layer hurt the performance of architecture then it will be skipped by regularization. So, this results in training a very deep neural network without the problems caused by vanishing/exploding gradients.

There is a similar approach called "**highway networks**", these networks also use skip connection. Similar to LSTM these skip connections also use parametric gates.

These gates determine how much information passes through the skip connection. This architecture however has not provided accuracy better than ResNet architecture.

Hence, ResNet uses Batch Normalization at its core. The Batch Normalization adjusts the input layer to increase the performance of the network. The problem of covariate shift is mitigated.ResNet makes use of the Identity Connection, which helps to protect the network from vanishing gradient problem.

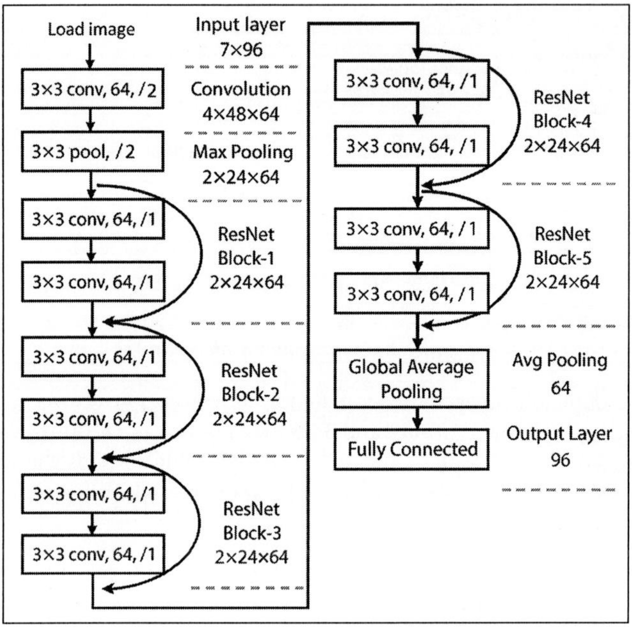

Figure 3.13: *Residual Network Architecture*

3.8 HYPER PARAMETER OPTIMIZATION

There are numerous parameters and layers in Deep neural networks. Calculating them and training the network with the parameters are difficult. Hence we need to optimize the hyper parameters.

The hyper parameters to be optimized are:

- **Learning rate:** Learning rate controls how much to update the weight in the optimization algorithm. To optimize it, use fixed learning rate, decrease learning rate, momentum based methods or adaptive learning rates depending on our choice of optimizer such as SGD.
- **Number epochs:** The number of times the entire training set passes through the neural network is called an epoch. Increase the epoch until the error becomes minimum.
- **Batch size:** ConvNet is sensitive to batch size. 16 to 128 batch size is a good choice.
- **Activation function:** Use activation functions such as ReLU and softmax to optimize.
- **Number of hidden layers and units:** When the neural network has less number of layers , it might lead to underfitting.
- **Weight initialization**
  - Initialize weight with a small random number to prevent dead neurons. But not too small a value to avoid zero gradient.
  - Uniform distribution works well.
- **Dropout:** Dropout probability of 0.5 is well suited for regularization.

3.9 NORMALIZATION

Normalization is a pre-processing technique used to standardize data. In other words, having different sources of data inside the same range. Not normalizing the data before training can cause problems in our network, making it drastically harder to train and decrease its learning speed.

There are two main methods to normalize our data. The most straightforward method is to scale it to a range from 0 to 1:

$$Xnormalised = x\text{-}m/XMAX\text{-}XMIN$$

X the data point to normalize, M the mean of the data set, X_{MAX} the highest value, and X_{MIN} the lowest value. This technique is generally used in the inputs of the data. The non-normalized data points with wide ranges can cause instability in Neural Networks. The relatively large inputs can cascade down to the layers, causing problems such as exploding gradients.

Intentionally Left Blank!

UNIT

4

Optimization and Generalization

4.1 OPTIMIZATION IN DEEP LEARNING

Deep learning is the subfield of machine learning which is used to perform complex tasks such as speech recognition, text classification, etc. A deep learning model consists of activation function, input, output, hidden layers, loss function, etc. Any deep learning model tries to generalize the data using an algorithm and tries to make predictions on the unseen data. We need an algorithm that maps the examples of inputs to that of the outputs and an optimization algorithm. An optimization algorithm finds the value of the parameters (weights) that minimize the error when mapping inputs to outputs. These optimization algorithms or optimizers widely affect the accuracy of the deep learning model. They as well as affect the speed training of the model.

While training the deep learning model, we need to modify each epoch's weights and minimize the loss function. An optimizer is a function or an algorithm that modifies the attributes of the neural network, such as weights and learning rate. Thus, it helps in reducing the overall loss and improves the accuracy.

Optimization Algorithms in Deep Learning

- Gradient Descent
- Stochastic Gradient Descent
- Stochastic Gradient descent with momentum
- Mini-Batch Gradient Descent
- Adagrad optimizer
- RMSProp optimizer
- AdaDelta optimizer
- Adam optimizer

Hyper Parameters of Optimization

- **Epoch:** The number of times the algorithm runs on the whole training dataset.
- **Sample**: A single row of a dataset.
- **Batch:** It denotes the number of samples to be taken for updating the model parameters.
- **Learning rate**: It is a parameter that provides the model a scale of how much model weights should be updated.

- **Cost Function/Loss Function**: A cost function is used to calculate the cost that is the difference between the predicted value and the actual value.
- **Weights/Bias:** The learnable parameters in a model that controls the signal between two neurons.

4.2 GRADIENT DESCENT DEEP LEARNING OPTIMIZER

Gradient Descent can be considered as the popular kid among the class of optimizers. This optimization algorithm uses calculus to modify the values consistently and to achieve the local minimum. In simple terms, consider you are holding a ball resting at the top of a bowl. When you lose the ball, it goes along the steepest direction and eventually settles at the bottom of the bowl. A Gradient provides the ball in the steepest direction to reach the local minimum that is the bottom of the bowl.

$$x\_new = x\text{-}alpha*f(x)$$

The above equation means how the gradient is calculated. Here alpha is step size that represents how far to move against each gradient with each iteration.

Gradient descent works as follows:

1. It starts with some coefficients, sees their cost, and searches for cost value lesser than what it is now.
2. It moves towards the lower weight and updates the value of the coefficients.
3. The process repeats until the local minimum is reached. A local minimum is a point beyond which it cannot proceed.

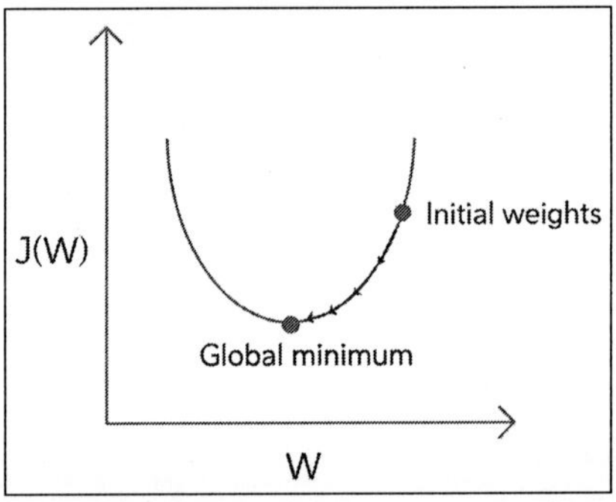

Figure 4.1: *Gradient Descent Works*

Gradient descent works best for most purposes. However, it has some downsides too. It is expensive to calculate the gradients if the size of the data is huge. Gradient descent workswell for convex functions but it doesn't know how far to travel along the gradient for nonconvex functions.

4.3 MINI BATCH GRADIENT DESCENT DEEP LEARNING OPTIMIZER

In this variant of gradient descent instead of taking all the training data, only a subset of the dataset is used for calculating the loss function. Since we are using a batch of data instead of taking the whole dataset, fewer iterations are needed. That is why the mini-batch gradient descent algorithm is faster than both stochastic gradient descent and batch gradient descent algorithms.

It needs a hyperparameter that is "mini-batch-size", which needs to be tuned to achieve the required accuracy. Although, the batch size of 32 is considered to be appropriate for almost every case. Also, in some cases, it results in poor final accuracy. Due to this, there needs a rise to look for other alternatives too

4.3.1 Stochastic Gradient Descent Deep Learning Optimizer

The term stochastic means randomness on which the algorithm is based upon. In stochastic gradient descent, instead of taking the whole dataset for each iteration, we randomly select the batches of data. That means we only take few samples from the dataset.

$$\omega := \omega - \eta \nabla Q_i(\omega)$$

where w is the weight, γ is the forgetting factor, ΔQ is the gradient.

The procedure is first to select the initial parameters w and learning rate n. Then randomly shuffle the data at each iteration to reach an approximate minimum.

Since we are not using the whole dataset but the batches of it for each iteration, the path taken by the algorithm is full of noise as compared to the gradient descent algorithm. Thus, SGD uses a higher number of iterations to reach the local minima. Due to an increase in the number of iterations, the overall computation time increases. But even after increasing the number of iterations, the computation cost is still less than that of the gradient descent optimizer. So, the conclusion is if the data is enormous and computational time is an essential factor, stochastic gradient descent should be preferred over batch gradient descent algorithm.

4.4 STOCHASTIC GRADIENT DESCENT WITH MOMENTUM DEEP LEARNING OPTIMIZER

Stochastic gradient descent takes a much noisier path than the gradient descent algorithm. Due to this reason, it requires a more significant number of iterations to reach the optimal minimum and hence computation time is very slow. To overcome the problem, we use stochastic gradient descent with a momentum algorithm.

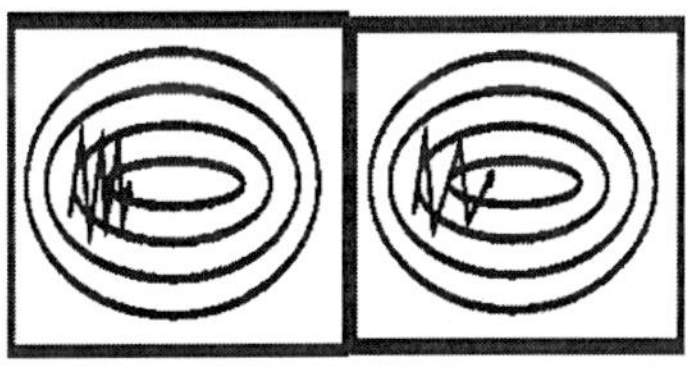

Figure 4.2: *Stochastic Gradient Descent with Momentum*

What the momentum does is helps in faster convergence of the loss function. Stochastic gradient descent oscillates between either direction of the gradient and updates the weights accordingly. However, adding a fraction of the previous update to the current update will make the process a bit faster. One thing that should be remembered while using this algorithm is that the learning rate should be decreased with a high momentum term.

In the above image, the left part shows the convergence graph of the stochastic gradient descent algorithm. At the same time, the right side shows SGD with momentum. From the image, you can compare the path chosen by both the algorithms and realize that using momentum helps reach convergence in less time. You might be thinking of using a large momentum and learning rate to make the process even faster. But remember that while increasing the momentum, the possibility of passing the optimal minimum also increases. This might result in poor accuracy and even more oscillations.

4.5 ADAGRAD (ADAPTIVE GRADIENT DESCENT) DEEP LEARNING OPTIMIZER

The adaptive gradient descent algorithm is slightly different from other gradient descent algorithms. This is because it uses different learning rates for each iteration. The change in learning rate depends upon the difference in the parameters during training. The more the parameters change, the more minor the learning rate changes. This modification is highly beneficial because real-world datasets contain sparse as well as dense features. So it is unfair to have the same value of learning rate for all the features. The Adagrad algorithm uses the below formula to update the weights. Here the $\alpha(t)$ denotes the different learning rates at each iteration, n is a constant, and E is a small positive to avoid division by 0.

$$w_t = w_t - 1 - \eta'_t \frac{\partial L}{\partial w(t-1)}$$

$$\eta^1_t = \frac{\eta}{\text{sqrt}(\alpha_t + \varepsilon)}$$

The benefit of using Adagrad is that it abolishes the need to modify the learning rate manually. It is more reliable than gradient descent algorithms and their variants, and it converges at a higher speed.

One downside of AdaGrad optimizer is that it decreases the learning rate aggressively and monotonically. There might be a point when the learning rate becomes extremely small. This is because the squared gradients in the denominator keep accumulating, and thus the denominator part keeps on increasing. Due to small learning rates, the model eventually becomes unable to acquire more knowledge, and hence the accuracy of the model is compromised.

4.6 RMS PROP(ROOT MEAN SQUARE) DEEP LEARNING OPTIMIZER

RMS prop is one of the popular optimizers among deep learning enthusiasts. This is maybe because it hasn't been published but still very well known in the community. RMS prop can also be considered an advancement in AdaGrad optimizer as it reduces the monotonically decreasing learning rate.

The algorithm mainly focuses on accelerating the optimization process by decreasing the number of function evaluations to reach the local minima. The algorithm keeps the moving average of squared gradients for every weight and divides the gradient by the square root of the mean square.

$$v(\omega,t) := \gamma v(\omega,t-1) + (1-\gamma)(\nabla Q_i(\omega))^2$$

where w is the weight, t is the time, v(w,t) is the moving average of the squared gradients, γ is the forgetting factor, Q is the gradient. Weights are updated by the below formula

$$\omega := \omega - \frac{\eta}{\sqrt{v(\omega,t)}} \nabla Q_i(\omega)$$

where η is the learning rate. In simpler terms, if there exists a parameter due to which the cost function oscillates a lot, we want to penalize the update of this parameter. The problem with RMS Prop is that the learning rate has to be defined manually and the suggested value doesn't work for every application.

4.7 ADADELTA DEEP LEARNING OPTIMIZER

AdaDelta can be seen as a more robust version of AdaGrad optimizer. It is based upon adaptive learning and is designed to deal with significant drawbacks of AdaGrad and RMS prop optimizer. The main problem with the above two optimizers is that the initial learning rate must be defined manually. One other problem is the decaying learning rate which becomes infinitesimally small at some point. Due to a certain number of iterations later, the model can no longer learn new knowledge.

To deal with these problems, AdaDelta uses two state variables to store the leaky average of the second moment gradient and a leaky average of the second moment of change of parameters in the model.

The running average **E[g²]t** at time step **t** then depends (as a fraction γ similarly to the Momentum term) only on the previous average and the current gradient value:

$$E\left[g^2\right]t = \gamma E[g^2]\mathrm{t}-1+(10-\gamma)g_t^2.$$

Next, we set γ to a similar value as the momentum term, say around 0.8. Update vector $\Delta\theta_t$:

$$\Delta, \quad = \eta \cdot g_{t,i}$$

$$\theta_{t+1} = \theta_t + \Delta\theta_t$$

The parameter update vector of Adagrad that we derived previously can also be written as shown below:

$$\Delta\theta = -\frac{\eta}{\sqrt{G_t + \varepsilon}} \odot g_t.$$

Now we can simply replace the diagonal matrix **Gt** with the decaying average over past squared gradients **E[g²]t** as shown below:

$$\Delta\theta_t = -\frac{\eta}{\sqrt{E[g^2]\mathrm{t}+\varepsilon}} g_t.$$

4.8 ADAM DEEP LEARNING OPTIMIZER

The name Adam is derived from adaptive moment estimation. This optimization algorithm is a further extension of stochastic gradient descent to update network weights during training. Unlike maintaining a single learning rate through training in SGD, Adam optimizer updates the learning rate for each network weight individually.

The Adam optimizer has several benefits, due to which it is used widely. It is adapted as a benchmark for deep learning papers and recommended as a default optimization algorithm. Moreover, the algorithm is straightforward to implement, has faster running time, low memory requirements, and requires less tuning than any other optimization algorithm.

$$m_t = \beta_1 m_{t-1} + (1 - \beta_1) \left[\frac{\delta L}{\delta w_t}\right] v_t = \beta_2 v_{t-1} + (1 - \beta_2) \left[\frac{\delta L}{\delta w_t}\right]^2$$

where,

mt = aggregate of gradients at time t [current] (initially, mt = 0) mt-1 = aggregate of gradients at time t-1 [previous]

Wt = weights at time t

L = derivative of Loss Function

Wt = derivative of weights at time t

β1 & β2 = Moving average parameter (const, 0.9)

4.9 NON-CONVEX OPTIMIZATION FOR DEEP NETWORKS

Non-Convex Optimization (NCO)

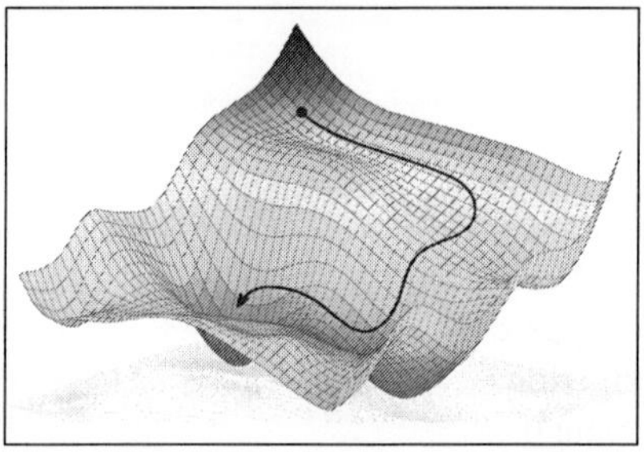

Figure 4.3: Non-Convex Optimization

NCO is a problem where the objective or any of the constraints are non-convex. Even simple looking problems with as few as ten variables can be extremely challenging, while problems with a few hundreds of variables can be intractable. Here, generally, we face the obligation to compromise, i.e,. give up seeking the optimal solution, which minimizes the objective over all feasible points. This compromise opens a door for local optimization where intensive research has been conducted and many developments were achieved. As a result, local optimization methods are widely used in applications where there is value in finding a good point, if not the very best. In an engineering design application, for example, local optimization can be used to improve the performance of a design originally obtained by manual, or other, design methods.

Limitations of Non-convex Optimization

- Optimization problems may have multiple feasible and very flat regions, a widely varying curvature, several saddle points, and multiple local minima within each region.
- It can then take time exponential in the number of variables and constraints to determine that a non-convex problem is infeasible, that the objective function is unbounded, or that an optimal solution is the global optimum across all feasible regions.
- The optimization may also require an initial guess, which is critical and can greatly affect the objective value of the local solution obtained.

Furthermore, little information is provided about how far from the global optimum the local solution is. Beyond this, local optimization methods are often sensitive to algorithm parameter values, which may need to be adjusted for a particular problem, or family of problems. To sum it up, roughly speaking, local optimization methods, used in non-convex optimization, are more art than technology. In contrast, except in some cases on the boundary of what is currently possible, there is little art involved in solving a least-squares problem or a linear program. Consequently, there cannot be a general algorithm to efficiently solve NCO problems in all cases and scenarios. NCP is then at least NP-hard. Weak theoretical guarantees add to the downsides of this type of optimization. However, it has the upside of an endless set of problems that we can try to solve better while learning more theoretical insights and improving the practical implementations.

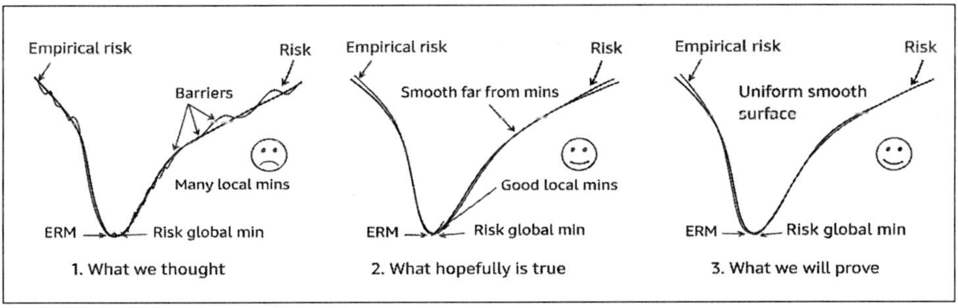

Figure 4.4: *Limitations of non-convex optimization Necessity of NCO*

NCO existed since the early days of operations research. Still, the topic gained more interest and focus with the emergence of DL in recent years. In fact, neural networks (NN)are universal function approximators. With enough neurons, they have the ability to approximate any function well. Among the functions to be approximated, non-convex functions are gaining more focus. To approximate them, convex functions cannot be good enough. Hence, the importance of using NCO increased. The freedom to express the learning problem as a non-convex optimization problem gives immense modeling power to the algorithm designer. Despite the guarantees achieved in individual instances, it is still complex to unify a framework of what makes NCO easy to control. On the practical side, conversations between theorists and practitioners can support the identification of what kind of conditions are rational for specific applications, and thus lead to the design of practically motivated algorithms for non-convex optimization with rigorous guarantees.

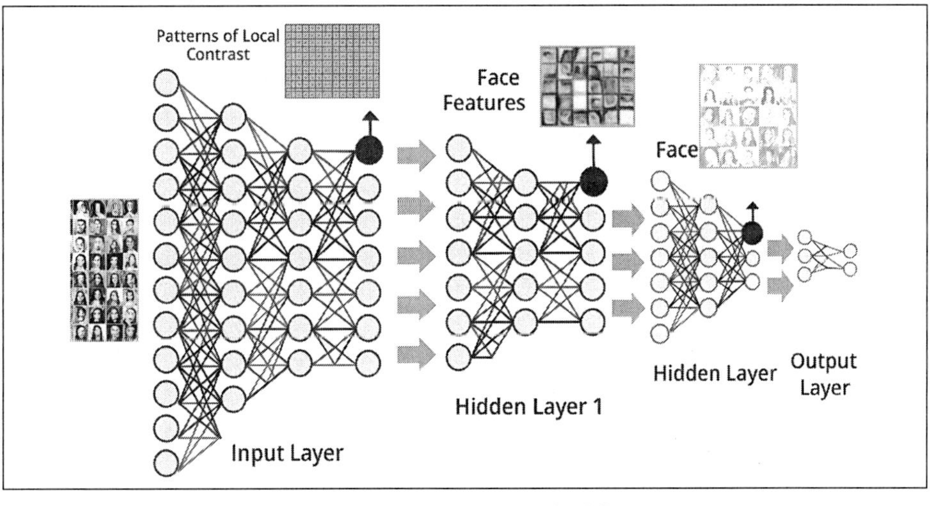

Figure 4.5: *Necessity of NCO*

Non-convex Optimization Convergence

For NCO, many CO techniques can be used such as stochastic gradient descent (SGD), mini-batching, stochastic variance-reduced gradient (SVRG), and momentum. There are also specialized methods for solving non-convex problems known in operations research such as alternating minimization methods, branch-and-bound methods. But these methods are not, generally, very popular for ML problems. In the same context, there are varieties of theoretical convergence results including convergence to a stationary point, convergence to a local minimum, local convergence to the global minimum, and global convergence to the global minimum.

As an example, let us consider the widely used SGD. Non-convex SGD converges with a slow theoretical rate, but not necessarily to a local minimum, which certainly means it doesn't necessarily reach the global optimum. These theoretical insights can be strengthened through the incorporation of stronger conditions and assumptions.

4.10 STOCHASTIC GRADIENT DESCENT (SGD)

SGD tries to solve the main problem in Batch Gradient descent which is the usage of whole training data to calculate gradients as each step. SGD is stochastic in nature i.e,. it picks up a "random" instance of training data at each step and then computes the gradient making it much faster as there is much fewer data to manipulate at a single time, unlikeBatch GD.

for i in range (m).

$$\theta j = \theta j - \alpha(y^i - y^i)X_j^i$$

The word "stochastic" means a system or process linked with a random probability. Hence, in Stochastic Gradient Descent, a few samples are selected randomly instead of the whole data set for the iteration. In Gradient Descent, there is a term called "batch" which denotes the total number of samples from a dataset that is used for calculating the gradient of the iteration.

4.11 GENERALIZATION IN NEURAL NETWORKS

One of the major advantages of neural nets is their ability to generalize. This means that a trained net could classify data from the same class as the learning data that it has never seen before. In real world applications developers normally have only a small part of all possible patterns for the generation of a neural net. To reach the best generalization, the dataset should be split into three parts:

- The **training set** is used to train a neural net. The error of this dataset is minimized during training.
- The **validation set** is used to determine the performance of a neural network on patterns that are not trained during learning.
- A **test set** for finally checking the overall performance of a neural net.

Dropout

This is one of the most interesting types of generalization techniques. It also produces very good results and is consequently the most frequently used regularization technique in the field of deep learning.

Dropout is a technique where randomly selected neurons are ignored during training. They are "dropped-out" randomly. This means that their contribution to the activation of downstream neurons is temporarily removed on the forward pass and any weight updates are not applied to the neuron on the backward pass.

Dropout may be implemented on any or all hidden layers in the network as well as the visible or input layer. It is not used on the output layer. Dropout regularization is a generic approach. The default interpretation of the dropout hyper parameter is the probability of training a given node in a layer, where 1.0 means no dropout, and 0.0 means no outputs from the layer. A good value for dropout in a hidden layer is between 0.5 and 0.8. Input layers use a larger dropout rate, such as 0.8.

Dropout is a regularization technique for reducing overfitting in neural networks by preventing complex co-adaptations on training data. It is a very efficient way of performing model averaging with neural networks. The term "dropout" refers to dropping out units (both hidden and visible) in a neural network.

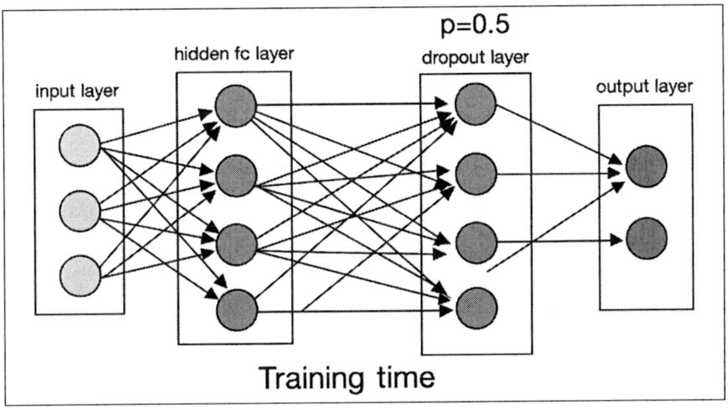

Figure 4.6: *Dropout Layer*

4.12 SPATIAL TRANSFORMER NETWORKS

Spatial Transformer modules, introduced by Max Jaderberg et al., are a popular way to increase spatial invariance of a model against spatial transformations such as translation, scaling, rotation, cropping, as well as non-rigid deformations. They can be inserted into existing convolutional architectures: either immediately following the input or in deeper layers.

The main benefit of this approach is that we now get two components with separate responsibilities: grid generator and sampler. The grid generator has the exclusive task of performing the inverse transformation and the sampler has the exclusive task of performing bilinear interpolation.

Grid Generator

The grid generator iterates over the regular grid of the output/target image and uses the inverse transformation T-1{...} to calculate the corresponding (usually non-integer) sample positions in the input/source image: the superscripts t and s are taken from the original paper and denote "target image" and "source image". The row and column indexes of the sampling grid are denoted as i and j, respectively. Please also note, that in the original paper the inverse transformation T-1{...} over the regular output grid is denoted as $\mathcal{T}_\theta(G)$.

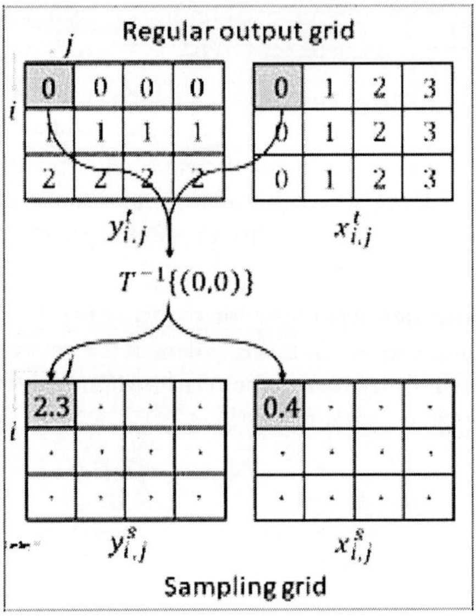

Figure 4.7: *Grid Generator*

Whereas in the above illustration the coordinates are calculated in a sequential manner for the sake of clarity, real world implementations of the grid generator will try to transform as many points as possible in parallel for reasons of computational efficiency.

The output of the grid generator is the so-called sampling grid, which is a set of points where the input map will be sampled to produce the spatially transformed output:

$$(y^S_{i,j,}x^S_{i,j})$$

where

$$0 \leq i \leq H' \qquad and\ 0 \leq j < W'$$

Please note that the size of the sampling grid determines the size of the target image.

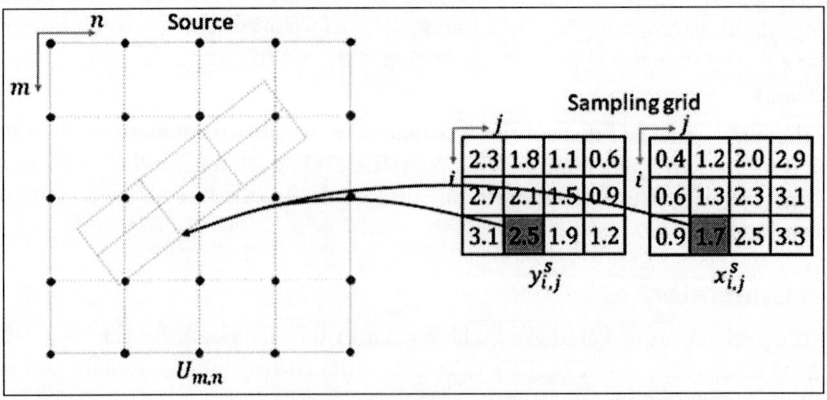

Figure 4.8: *Sampling Grid*

Sampler

The sampler iterates over the entries of the sampling grid and extracts the corresponding pixel values from the input map using bilinear interpolation:

The extraction of a pixel value consists of three operations:

- find the four neighboring points (upper left, upper right, lower left and lower right)
- for each neighboring point calculate its corresponding weight
- take the weighted average to produce the output.

Localisation Net

The task of the localisation network is to find parameters θ of the inverse transformation T-1{...}, which puts the input feature map to a canonical pose, thus simplify recognition in the following layers. The localisation network can take any form, such as a fully-connected network or a convolutional network, but should include a final regression layer to produce the transformation parameters θ:

The size of θ can vary depending on the transformation that is parameterized, e.g,. for an affine transformation θ is 6-dimensional:

The affine transform is quite powerful and contains translation, scaling, rotation and shearing as special cases. For many tasks however a simpler transformation may be sufficient, e.g,. a pure translation is implemented using only 2 parameters:

$$\begin{bmatrix} x_{i,j}^{s} \\ y_{i,j}^{s} \end{bmatrix} = T^{-1}\left\{\begin{bmatrix} x_{i,j}^{t} \\ y_{i,j}^{t} \end{bmatrix}\right\} = \begin{bmatrix} x_{i,j}^{t} \\ y_{i,j}^{t} \end{bmatrix} + \begin{bmatrix} \theta_1 \\ \theta_2 \end{bmatrix}$$

Both the grid generator and the sampler are parameter less operations, i.e,. they don't have any trainable parameters. In this regard they are comparable to a max-pooling layer. The brainpower of a spatial transformer module hence comes from the localisation net, which must learn to detect the pose of the input feature map (such as its orientation, scale etc.) in order to produce an appropriate transformation.

The input feature map U is first passed to the localisation network, which regresses the appropriate transformation parameters θ. The grid generator then uses the transformation parameters θ to produce the sampling grid, which is a set of points where the input feature map shall be sampled. Finally, the sampler takes both the input feature map and the sampling grid and using e.g,. bilinear interpolation outputs the transformed feature map.

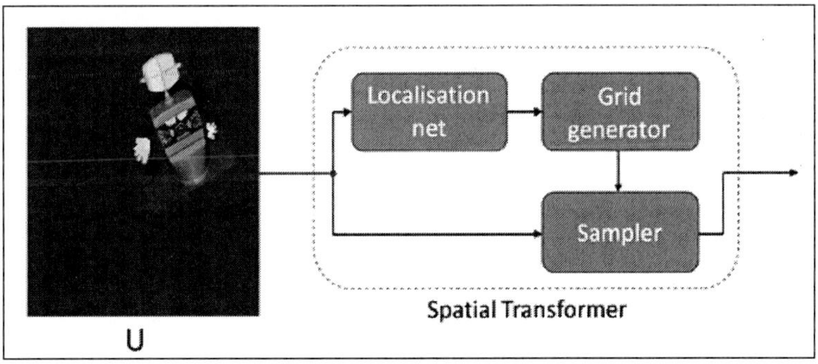

Figure 4.9: *Spatial Transformer*

4.13 RECURRENT NETWORKS (RNN)

RNN works on the principle of saving the output of a particular layer and feeding this back to the input in order to predict the output of the layer.

$$\begin{bmatrix} x_{i,j}^{s} \\ y_{i,j}^{s} \end{bmatrix} = T^{-1}\left\{\begin{bmatrix} x_{i,j}^{t} \\ y_{i,j}^{t} \end{bmatrix}\right\} = \begin{bmatrix} \theta_1 & \theta_2 \\ \theta_3 & \theta_4 \end{bmatrix} \cdot \begin{bmatrix} x_{i,j}^{t} \\ y_{i,j}^{t} \end{bmatrix} + \begin{bmatrix} \theta_5 \\ \theta_6 \end{bmatrix}$$

Below is how you can convert a Feed-Forward Neural Network into a Recurrent NeuralNetwork:

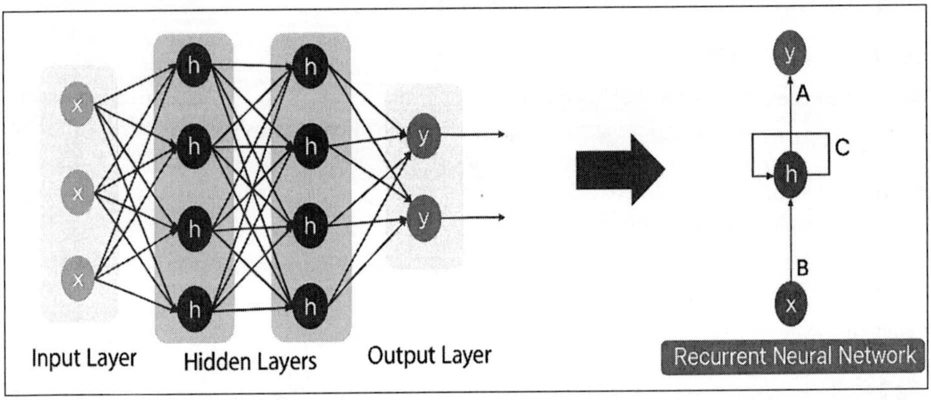

Figure 4.10: *Simple Recurrent Neural Network*

The nodes in different layers of the neural network are compressed to form a single layer of recurrent neural networks. A, B, and C are the parameters of the network.

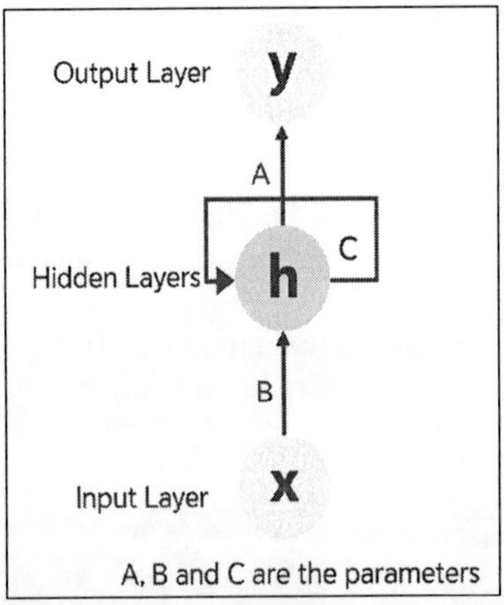

Figure 4.11: *Fully connected Recurrent Neural Network*

Here, "x" is the input layer, "h" is the hidden layer, and "y" is the output layer. A, B, and C are the network parameters used to improve the output of the model. At any given time t, the current input is a combination of input at x(t) and x(t-1). The output at any given time is fetched back to the network to improve on the output.

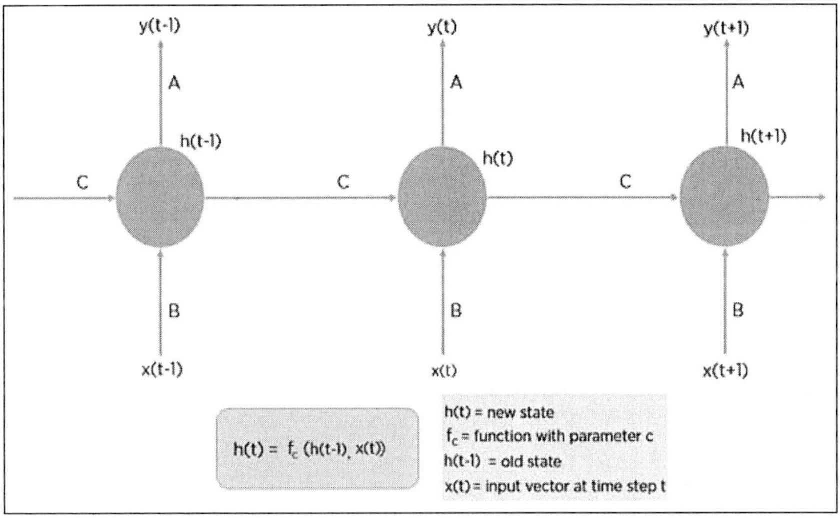

Figure 4.12: *Fully connected Recurrent Neural Network*

Now that you understand what a recurrent neural network is let's look at the different types of recurrent neural networks.

4.14 RNN LANGUAGE MODELLING

RNN were created because there were a few issues in the feed-forward neural network:

- Cannot handle sequential data
- Considers only the current input
- Cannot memorize previous inputs

The solution to these issues is the RNN. An RNN can handle sequential data, accepting the current input data, and previously received inputs. RNNs can memorize previous inputs due to their internal memory.

How Does Recurrent Neural Networks Work?

In Recurrent Neural networks, the information cycles through a loop to the middle-hidden layer.

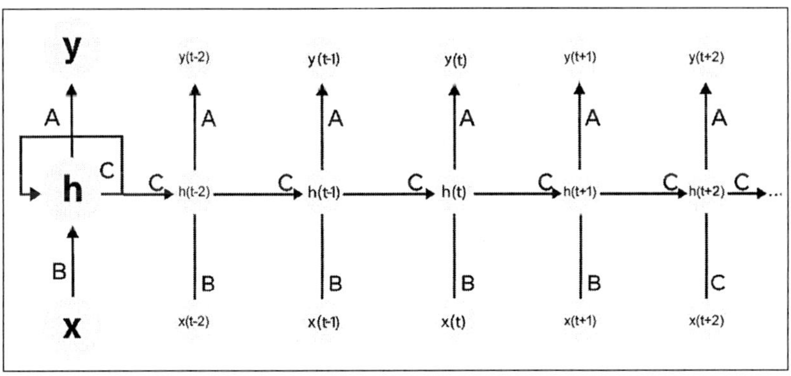

Figure 4.13: *Working of Recurrent Neural Network*

The input layer "x" takes in the input to the neural network and processes it and passes it on the middle layer.

The middle layer "h" can consist of multiple hidden layers, each with its own activation functions and weights and biases. If you have a neural network where the various parameters of different hidden layers are not affected by the previous layer, ie,. the neural network does not have memory, then you can use a recurrent neural network.

The Recurrent Neural Network will standardize the different activation functions and weights and biases so that each hidden layer has the same parameters. Then, instead of creating multiple hidden layers, it will create one and loop over it as many times as required.

Feed-Forward Neural Networks vs Recurrent Neural Networks

A feed-forward neural network allows information to flow only in the forward direction, from the input nodes, through the hidden layers, and to the output nodes. There are no cycles or loops in the network.

Below is how a simplified presentation of a feed-forward neural network looks like:

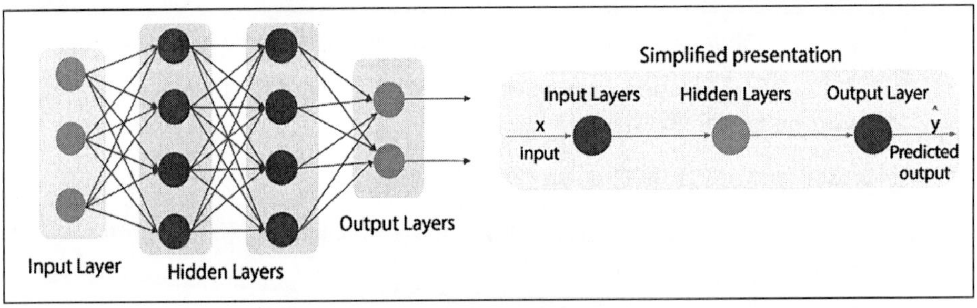

Figure 4.14: *Feed-forward Neural Network*

In a feed-forward neural network, the decisions are based on the current input. It doesn't memorize the past data, and there's no future scope. Feed-forward neural networks are used in general regression and classification problems.

Applications of Recurrent Neural Networks

- Image Captioning
- Time Series Prediction
- Any time series problem, like predicting the prices of stocks in a particular month, can be solved using an RNN.
- Natural Language Processing
- Text mining and Sentiment analysis can be carried out using an RNN for NaturalLanguage Processing (NLP).
- Machine Translation

Types of Recurrent Neural Networks

There are four types of Recurrent Neural Networks:

- One to One
- One to Many

- Many to One
- Many to Many

One to One RNN

This type of neural network is known as the Vanilla Neural Network. It's used for general machine learning problems, which has a single input and a single output.

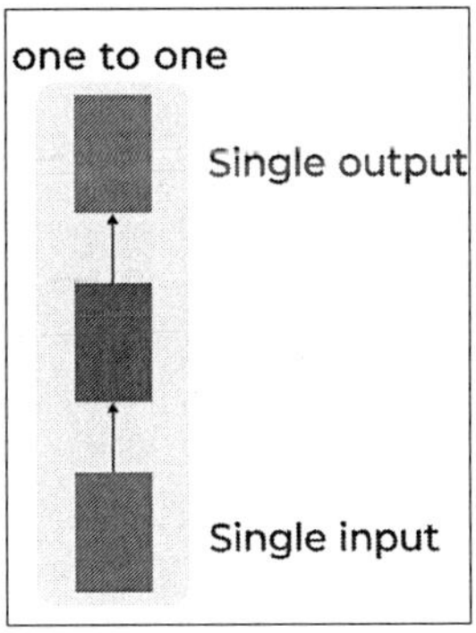

Figure 4.15: *One to One RNN*

One to Many RNN

This type of neural network has a single input and multiple outputs. An example of this is the image caption.

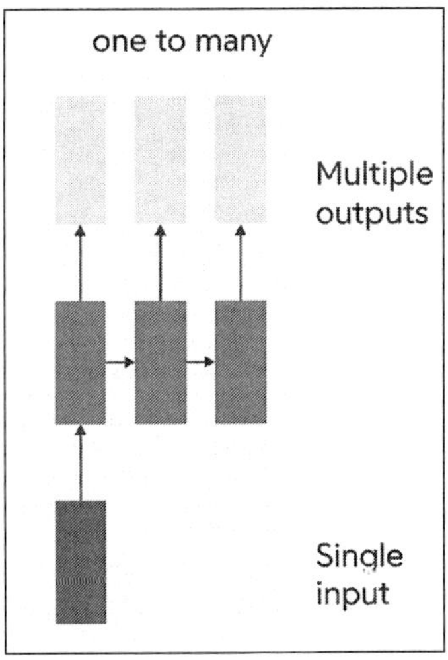

Figure 4.16: *One to Many RNN*

Many to One RNN

This RNN takes a sequence of inputs and generates a single output. Sentiment analysis is a good example of this kind of network where a given sentence can be classified as expressing positive or negative sentiments.

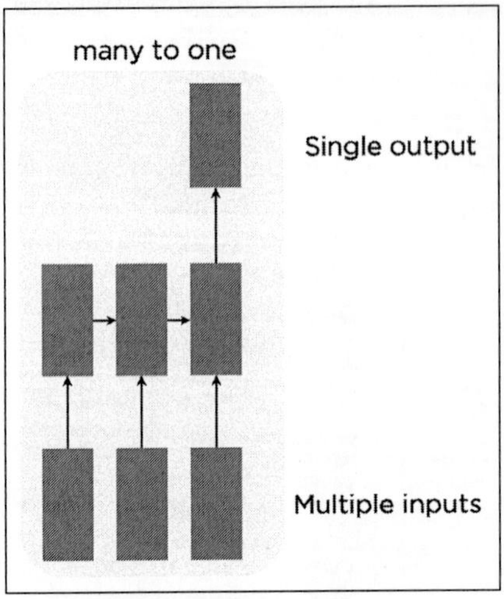

Figure 4.17: *Many to One RNN*

Many to Many RNN

This RNN takes a sequence of inputs and generates a sequence of outputs. Machine Translation is one of the examples.

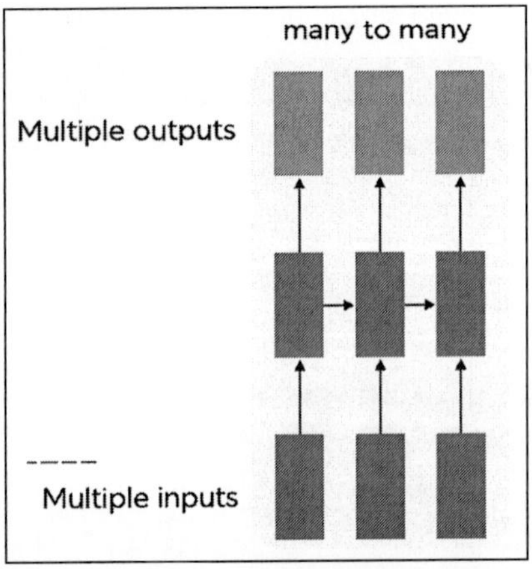

Figure 4.18: *Many to Many RNN*

Two Issues of Standard RNNs

1. Vanishing Gradient Problem

Recurrent Neural Networks enable you to model time-dependent and sequential data problems, such as stock market prediction, machine translation, and text generation. You will find, however, RNN is hard to train because of the gradient problem.

RNNs suffer from the problem of vanishing gradients. The gradients carry information used in the RNN, and when the gradient becomes too small, the parameter updates become insignificant. This makes the learning of long data sequences difficult.

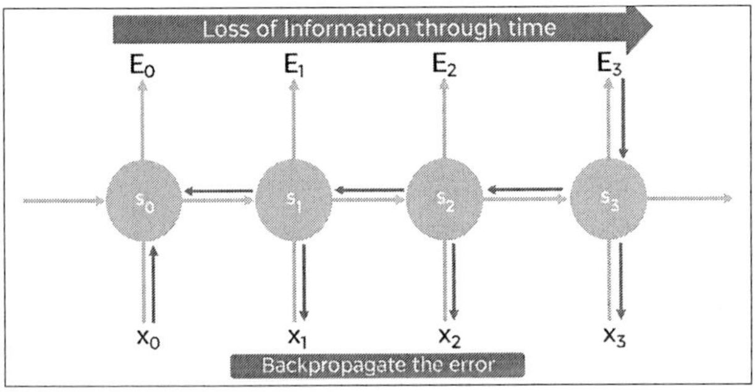

Figure 4.19: *Vanishing Gradient Problem*

2. Exploding Gradient Problem

While training a neural network, if the slope tends to grow exponentially instead of decaying, this is called an Exploding Gradient. This problem arises when large error gradients accumulate, resulting in very large updates to the neural network model weights during the training process. Long training time, poor performance, and bad accuracy are the major issues in gradient problems.

4.15 LONG SHORT TERM MEMORY LSTM

Long Short Term Memory Network is an advanced RNN, a sequential network, that allows information to persist. It is capable of handling the vanishing gradient problem faced by RNN. A recurrent neural network also known as RNN is used for persistent memory.

- LSTM is a special kind of recurrent neural network capable of handling long-term dependencies.
- Understand the architecture and working of an LSTM network

Long Short Term Memory Network is an advanced RNN, a sequential network that allows information to persist. It is capable of handling the vanishing gradient problem faced by RNN. A recurrent neural network also known as RNN is used for persistent memory.

At a high-level LSTM works very much like an RNN cell. Here is the internal functioning of the LSTM network. The LSTM consists of three parts, as shown in the image below and each part performs an individual function.

Structure of LSTM

LSTM has a chain structure that contains four neural networks and different memory blocks called **cells.**

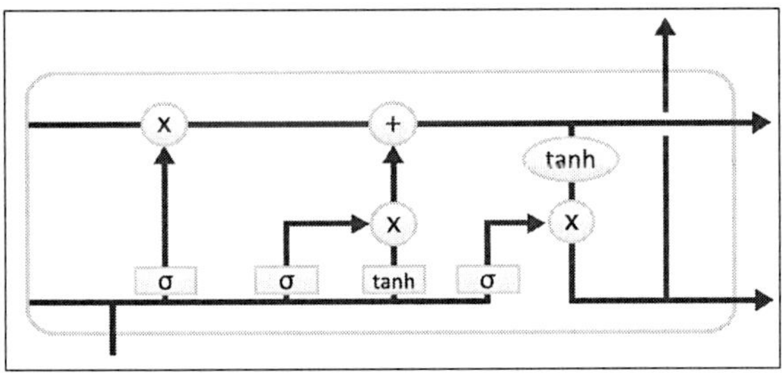

Figure 4.20: *Structure of LSTM*

Information is retained by the cells and the memory manipulations are done by the **gates.** There are three gates:

Forget Gate

The information that is no longer useful in the cell state is removed with the forget gate. Two inputs *x_t* (input at the particular time) and *h_t-1* (previous cell output) are fed to the gate and multiplied with weight matrices followed by the addition of bias. The resultant is passed through an activation function which gives a binary output. If for a particular cell state the output is 0, the piece of information is forgotten and for output 1, the information is retained for future use.

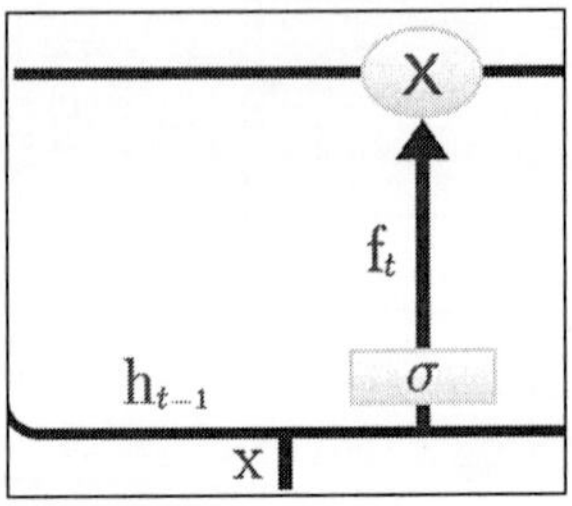

Figure 4.21: *Forget Gate*

Input Gate

The addition of useful information to the cell state is done by the input gate. First, the information is regulated using the sigmoid function and filter the values to be remembered similar to the forget gate using inputs *h_t-1* and *x_t*. Then, a vector is created using *tanh* function that gives an output from -1 to +1, which contains all the possible values from h_t-1 and *x_t*. At last, the values of the vector and the regulated values are multiplied to obtain the useful information.

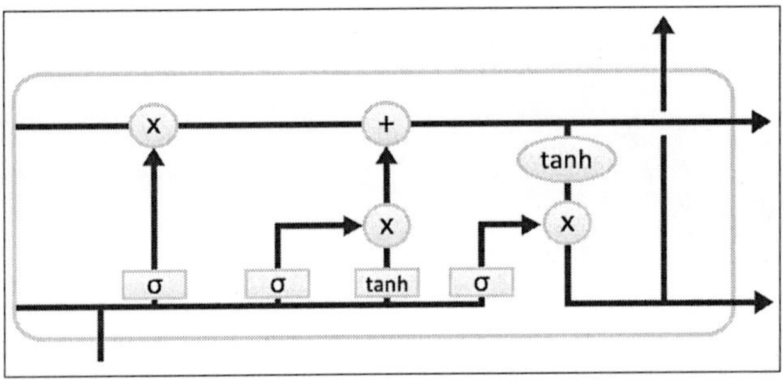

Figure 4.22: *Input Gate*

Output Gate

The task of extracting useful information from the current cell state to be presented as output is done by the output gate. First, a vector is generated by applying tanh function on the cell. Then, the information is regulated using the sigmoid function and filtered by the values to be remembered using inputs *h_t-1* and *x_t*. At last, the values of the vector and the regulated values are multiplied to be sent as an output and input to the next cell.

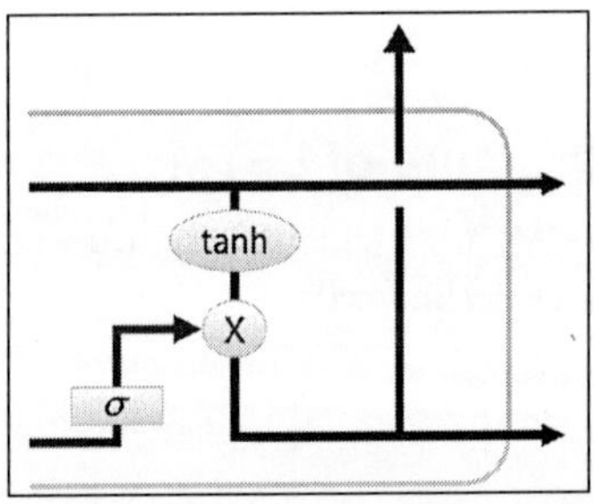

Figure 4.23: *Output Gate Some of the famous applications of LSTM includes*

1. Language Modelling
2. Machine Translation
3. Image Captioning
4. Handwriting generation
5. Question Answering Chatbots

4.16 DEEP REINFORCEMENT LEARNING

- Reinforcement Learning directly takes inspiration from how human beings learn from data in their lives. It features an algorithm that improves upon itself and learns from new situations using a trial-and- error method.
- Favourable outputs are encouraged or "reinforced", and non-favourable outputs are discouraged or "punished".
- In every iteration of the algorithm, the output result is given to the interpreter, which decides whether the outcome is favourable or not.
- In case of the program finding the correct solution, the interpreter reinforces the solution by providing a reward to the algorithm. If the outcome is not favourable, thc algorithm is forced to reiterate until it finds a better result. In most cases, the reward system is directly tied to the effectiveness of the result.
- In typical reinforcement learning use-cases, such as finding the shortest route between two points on a map, the solution is not an absolute value. Instead, it takes on a score of effectiveness, expressed in a percentage value. The higher this percentage value is,the more reward is given to the algorithm.
- Thus, the program is trained to give the best possible solution for the best possible reward.

Reinforcement Learning Applications

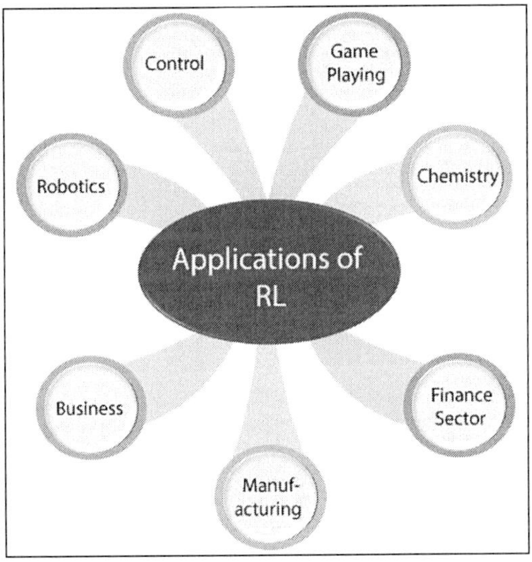

Figure 4.24: *Reinforcement Learning Applications*

Types of Reinforcement Learning

There are mainly two types of reinforcement learning, which are:

Positive Reinforcement

The positive reinforcement learning means adding something to increase the tendency that expected behaviour would occur again. It impacts positively on the behaviour of the agent and increases the strength of the behaviour. This type of reinforcement can sustain the changes for a long time, but too much positive reinforcement may lead to an overload of states that can reduce the consequences.

Negative Reinforcement

The negative reinforcement learning is opposite to the positive reinforcement as it increases the tendency that the specific behaviour will occur again by avoiding the negative condition. It can be more effective than the positive reinforcement depending on the situation and behaviour, but it provides reinforcement only to meet minimum behaviour.

4.17 COMPUTATIONAL & ARTIFICIAL NEUROSCIENCE

A neural network is a method in artificial intelligence that teaches computers to process data in a way that is inspired by the human brain. It is a type of machine learning process, called deep learning, that uses interconnected nodes or neurons in a layered structure that resembles the human brain.

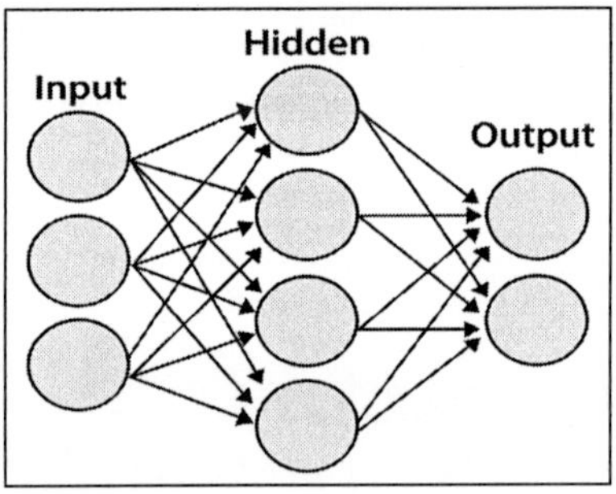

Figure 4.25: *Neural Network*

Neuroscience examines the structure and function of the human brain and nervous system. Neuroscientists use cellular and molecular biology, anatomy and physiology, human behavior and cognition, and other disciplines, to map the brain at a mechanistic level.

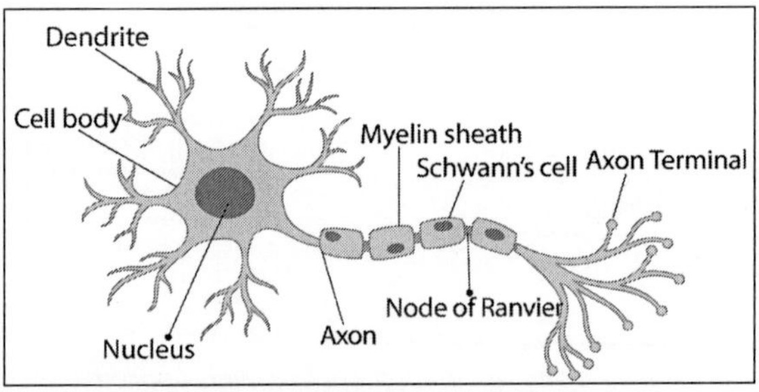

Figure 4.26: *Neuroscience*

The collaboration between artificial intelligence and neuroscience can produce an understanding of the mechanisms in the brain that generate human cognition. This article reviews multidisciplinary research lines that could achieve this understanding. Artificial intelligence has an important role to play in research, because artificial intelligence focuses on the mechanisms that generate intelligence and cognition.

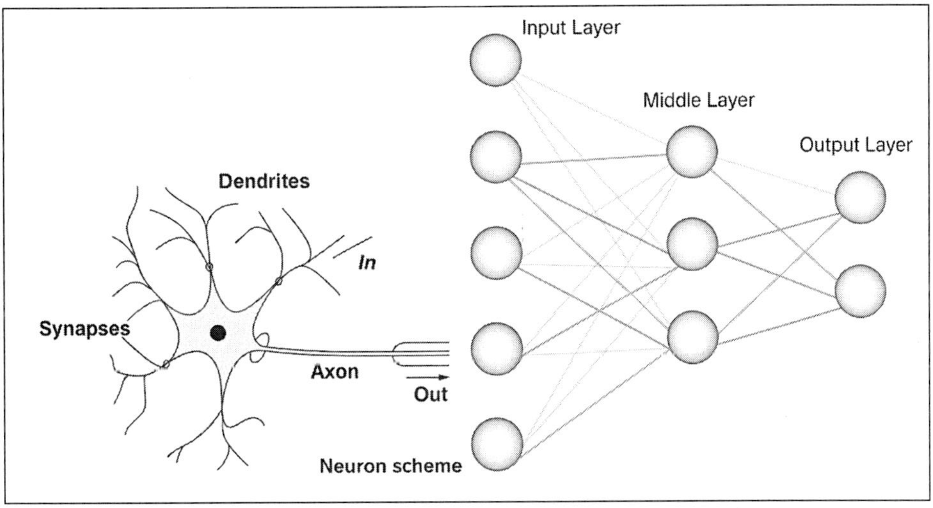

Figure 4.27: *The Collaboration Between Artificial Intelligence and Neuroscience*

Intentionally Left Blank!

UNIT

5

Case Study and Applications

5.1 IMAGENET

It is an image database organized according to the WordNet hierarchy, in which each node of the hierarchy is depicted by hundreds and thousands of images. The project has been instrumental in advancing computer vision and deep learning research. The data is available for free to researchers for non- commercial use.

The most highly-used subset of ImageNet is the ImageNet Large Scale Visual Recognition Challenge (ILSVRC) 2012-2017 image classification and localization dataset.

This dataset spans 1000 object classes and contains 12,81,167 training images, 50,000 validation images and 1,00,000 test images.

Each meaningful concept in WordNet, possibly described by multiple words or word phrases, is called a "synonym set" or "synset".

There are more than 1,00,000 synsets in WordNet; the majority of them are nouns (80,000+). In ImageNet, we aim to provide on average 1000 images to illustrate each synset. Images of each concept are quality-controlled and human- annotated. In its completion, ImageNet will offer tens of millions of cleanly labeled and sorted images for most of the concepts in the WordNet hierarchy.

Need for ImageNet in Computer Vision

The ImageNet project was inspired by two important needs in computer vision research.

1. The first was the need to establish a clear North Star problem in computer vision. While the field enjoyed an abundance of important tasks to work on, from stereo vision to image retrieval, from 3D reconstruction to image segmentation, object categorization was recognized to be one of the most fundamental capabilities of both human and machine vision. Hence there was a growing demand for a high quality object categorization benchmark with clearly established evaluation metrics.
2. There was a critical need for more data to enable more generalizable machine learning methods. Ever since the birth of the digital era and the availability of web-scale data exchanges, researchers in these fields have been working hard to design more and more sophisticated algorithms to index, retrieve, organize and annotate multimedia data.

But good research requires good resources. To tackle this problem at scale, it was critical to provide researchers with a large-scale image database for both training and testing. The convergence of these two intellectual reasons motivated to build ImageNet.

5.2 AUDIO WAVENET

WaveNet is a type of feedforward neural network known as a deep convolutional neural network (CNN). In WaveNet, the CNN takes a raw audio signal as an input and synthesizes an output one sample at a time.

The joint probability of a waveform **x** = {x1,x2,....xn} is factorized as a product of conditional probabilities as follows:

$$p(\mathbf{x}) = \prod_{t=1}^{T} p(x_t \mid x_1, \ldots, x_{t-1})$$

Each audio sample x_t is therefore conditioned on the samples at all previous timesteps.

There are no pooling layers in the network, and the output of the model has the same time dimensionality as the input. The model outputs a categorical distribution over the next value x_t with a softmax layer and it is optimized to maximize the log likelihood of the data with respect to the parameters. Because log-likelihoods are tractable, we tune hyperparameters on a validation set and can easily measure if the model is overfitting or underfitting.

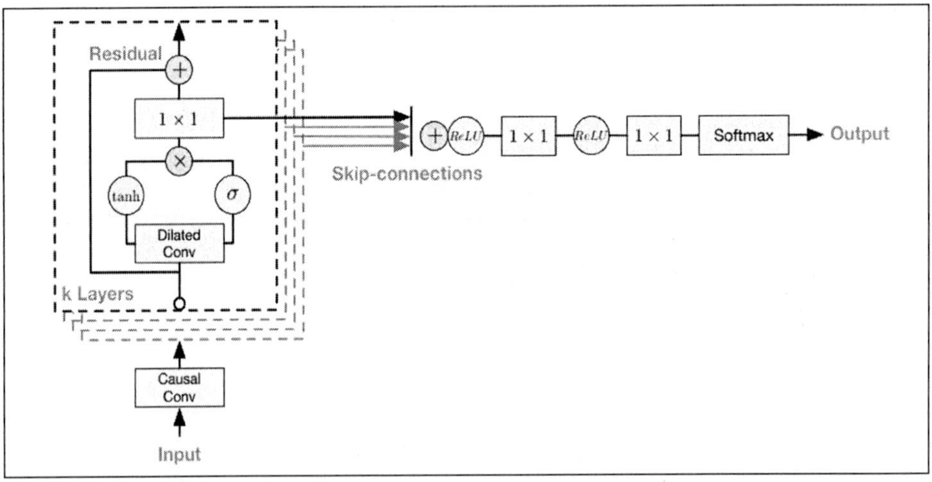

***Figure 5.1**: Architecture of WaveNet*

5.2.1 Causal Convolutions

The main ingredient of WaveNet are causal convolutions. By using causal convolutions, we make sure the model cannot violate the ordering in which we model the data: the prediction p $(x_{t+1} \mid x_1, ..., x_t)$ emitted by the model at timestep, t cannot depend on any of the future timesteps $x_{t+1}, x_{t+2}, \ldots, x_T$

At training time, the conditional predictions for all timesteps can be made in parallel because all timesteps of ground truth x are known. When generated with the model, the predictions are sequential: after each sample is predicted, it is fed back into the network to predict the next sample.

One of the problems of causal convolutions is that they require many layers, or large filters to increase the receptive field. For example, in the figure the receptive field is only 5 (= #layers + filter length - 1).

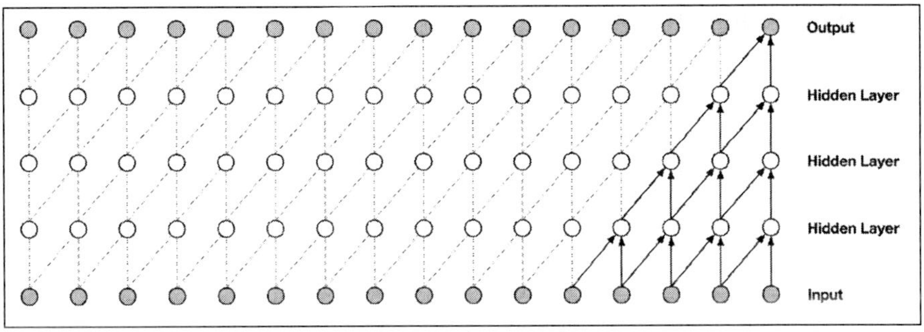

Figure 5.2: *Visualization of a stack of causal convolutional layers*

5.2.2 Dilated Causal Convolutions

A dilated convolution is a convolution where the filter is applied over an area larger than its length by skipping input values with a certain step. Dilated convolution with dilation 1 yields the standard convolution. Figure 5.3 depicts dilated causal convolutions for dilations 1, 2, 4, and 8.

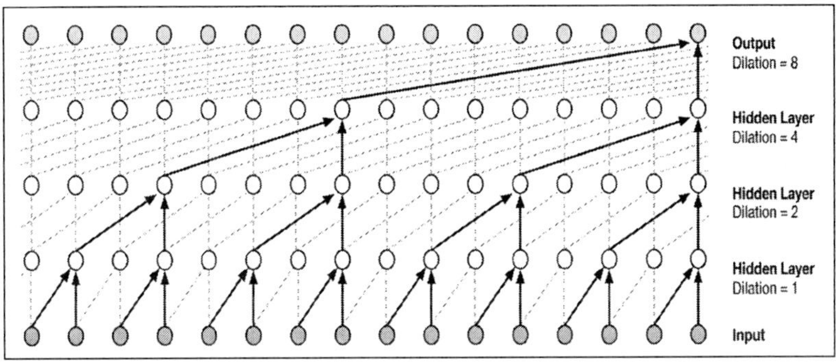

Figure 5.3: *Visualization of a stack of dilated causal convolutional layers*

Stacked dilated convolutions enable networks to have very large receptive fields with just a few layers, while preserving the input resolution throughout the network as well as computational efficiency.

5.2.3 Softmax Distributions

Because raw audio is typically stored as a sequence of 16-bit integer values (one per timestep), a softmax layer would need to output 65,536 probabilities per timestep to model all possible values. To make this more tractable, we first apply a μ-law companding transformation to the data, and then quantize it to 256 possible values:

$$f(x_t) = \text{sign}(x_t)\frac{\ln(1 + \mu|x_t|)}{\ln(1 + \mu)},$$

where $-1 < x_t < 1$ and $\mu = 255$

5.2.4 Gated Activation Units

The gated activation unit is given by the formula

$$\mathbf{z} = \tanh(W_{f,k} * \mathbf{x}) \odot \sigma(W_{g,k} * \mathbf{x})$$

where $*$ denotes a convolution operator, $\odot$ denotes an element-wise multiplication operator, $\sigma(\cdot)$ is a sigmoid function, k is the layer index, f and g denote filter and gate, respectively, and W is a learnable convolution filter.

5.2.5 Conditional Wavenets

Given an additional input h, WaveNets can model the conditional distribution p (x | h) of the audio given this input.

$$p(\mathbf{x} \mid \mathbf{h}) = \prod_{t=1}^{T} p(x_t \mid x_1, \ldots, x_{t-1}, \mathbf{h}) .$$

In a multi-speaker setting we can choose the speaker by feeding the speaker identity to the model as an extra input. Similarly, for Text-to-speech (TTS) we need to feed information about the text as an extra input.

WaveNets produced samples that outperform the current best TTS systems in subjective naturalness. WaveNets showed very promising results when applied to music audio modeling and speech recognition.

Applications of Wavenet

WaveNet was then used to generate Google Assistant voices for US English and Japanese across all Google platforms.

WaveNet greatly reduced the number of audio recordings that were required to create a voice model by modeling the raw audio of the voice actor samples

5.3 NATURAL LANGUAGE PROCESSING - WORD2VEC

NLP is the ability of computers to understand text and spoken words in much the same way human beings can. NLP combines computational linguistics—rule- based modeling of human language—with statistical, machine learning, and deep learning models. Together, these technologies enable computers to process human language in the form of text or voice data and to 'understand' its full meaning, complete with the speaker or writer's intent and sentiment. NLP drives computer programs that translate text from one language to another, respond to spoken commands, and summarize large volumes of text rapidly— even in real time.

Use case of NLP

- Speech recognition
- Part of speech tagging
- Word sense disambiguation
- Coreference resolution
- Sentiment analysis
- Natural language generation

Word Embedding – Word2Vec

Word embedding is a way of representing words as vectors. These models are widely used in NLP problems. The main goal of word embedding is to convert the high dimensional feature space of words into low dimensional feature vectors by preserving the contextual similarity in the corpus. It first generates a vocabulary with the help of a training text corpus (input) and then learns the word embedding representations word vectors (output). Language modeling technique used for mapping words to vectors of real numbers. Word embeddings can be generated using various methods like neural networks, co- occurrence matrices, probabilistic models, etc. They can be used as feature vectors for the Machine Learning model, used to measure text similarity using cosine similarity techniques, words clustering, and text classification techniques

The popular pre-trained models to create word embedding of a text are as follows:

- **Word2Vec** — From Google
- **Fast text** — From Facebook
- **Glove** — From Stanford

The Word2Vec model is used for Word representations in Vector Space. It was founded by Tomas Mikolov and a group of the research teams from Google in 2013. It is a neural network model that attempts to explain the word embeddings based on a text corpus.

To label how words are similar or close to each other, we first fix the window size, which determines which nearby words we want to pick.

For Example, For a window size of 2, implies that for every word, we'll pick the 2 words behind and the 2 words after it. Let's see the following example:

sentence : the pink horse is eating	
Sentence	**Word pairs**
the pink horse is eating	(**the**, pink), (**the**, horse)
the **pink** horse is eating	(**pink**, the), (**pink**, horse), (**pink**, is)
the pink **horse** is eating	(**horse**, the), (**horse**, pink), (**horse**, is), (**horse**, eating)
the pink horse **is** eating	(**is**, pink), (**is**, horse), (**is**, eating)
the pink horse is **eating**	(**eating**, horse), (**eating**, is)

Word2Vec Algorithm

Step-1: Initially assign a vector of random numbers to each word in the corpus.

Step-2: Then, iterate through each word of the document and grab the vectors of the nearest n-words on either side of our target word, and concatenate all these vectors, and then forward propagate these concatenated vectors through a **linear layer + softmax function**, and try to predict what our target word was.

Step-3: In this step, we will compute the error between our estimate and the actual target word and then back propagate the error and then modify not only the weights of the linear layer but also the vectors or embeddings of our neighbour's words.

Step-4: Finally, we will extract the weights from the hidden layer and by using these weights encode the meaning of words in the vocabulary.

Example: Vector("King") - Vector("Man") + Vector("Woman") = Word("?") Answer: Vector("King")-Vector("Man")+ Vector("Woman") = Word ("Queen")

Proof

Consider the following attributes for different characters in a kingdom:

	Battle	Horse	King	Man	Queen	....	Woman
Authority						....	
Event						....	
Has tail						....	
rich						....	
gender						....	

To fill the attribute values randomly find suitable values, For Example; the king values can be represented as,

King [Authority = 1 (He is the authorized person of the kingdom) , Has tail = 0 (He doesn't have a tail), Rich = 1 (A king is always rich), Gender = -1 (For male =-1 & Female = 1). Therefore the word King Can be represented in vectors as KING [1,0,1,-1]

In the same way comparing each attributes and and assigning values.

	Battle	Horse	King	Man	Queen	....	Woman
Authority	0	0.01	1	0.2	1	....	0.2
Event	1	0	0	0	0	....	0
Has tail	0	1	0	0	0	....	0
rich	0	0.1	1	0.3	1	....	0.2
gender	0	1	-1	-1	1	....	1

Now equate the vector values for "King – Man + woman = ?"

King		Man		Woman		?
1		0.2		0.2		1
0		0		0		0
0	–	0	+	0	=	0
1		0.3		0.2		0.9
–1		–1		1		1

We got The answer vector as [1,0,0,0.9,1] = [1,0,0,1,1] == Queen. So,

Vector("King") - Vector("Man") +Vector("Woman") = Word("Queen")

Preprocessing Modules in Word2Vec

1. Continuous Bag of Words (CBOW)
2. Skip-Gram

Continuous Bag of Words (CBOW)

CBOW (Continuous Bag of Words): CBOW model predicts the current word given context words within a specific window. The input layer contains the context words and the output layer contains the current word. The hidden layer contains the number of dimensions in which we want to represent the current word present at the output layer. The aim of the CBOW model is to predict a target word in its neighborhood, using all words. To predict the target word, this model uses the sum of the background vectors. For this, we use the pre-defined window size surrounding the target word to define the neighboring terms that are taken into account.

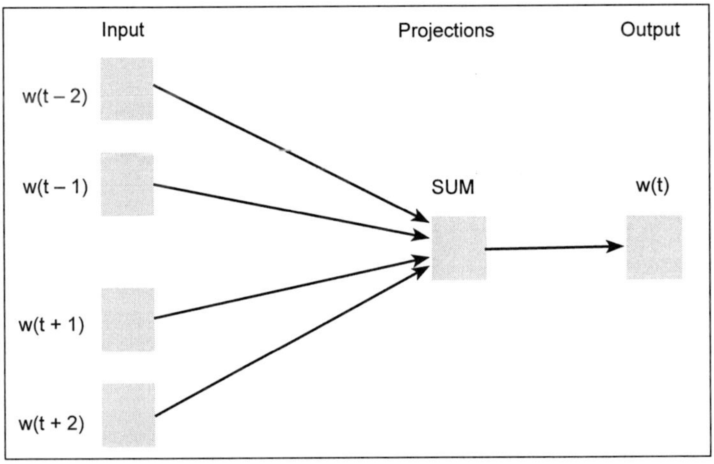

Figure 5.4: *Continuous Bag of words*

Skip Gram

- Skip gram predicts the surrounding context words
- Within a specific window given the current word.
- The input layer contains the current word and the output layer contains the context words.
- The hidden layer contains the number of dimensions in which we want to represent the current word present at the input layer.

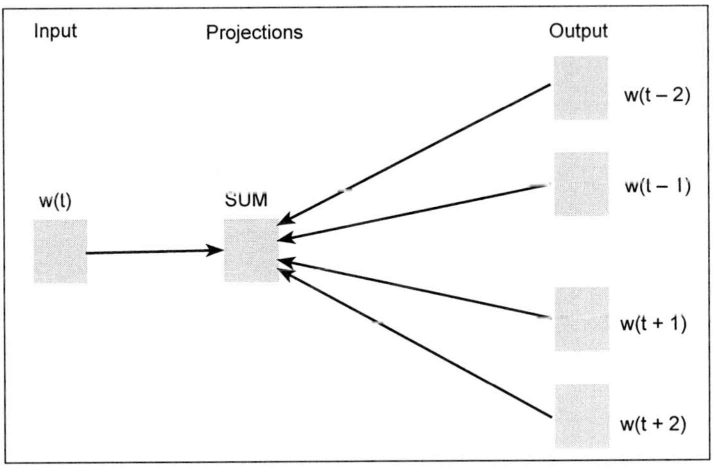

Figure 5.5: *Skip Gram*

CBOW Vs Skip Gram

- The Skip-Gram model works well with a small amount of the training datasets, and can better represent rare words or phrases.
- CBOW model is observed to train faster than Skip Gram, and can better
- represent more frequent words which mean gives slightly better accuracy for the frequent words.

Applications of Word Embedding

- Sentiment Analysis
- Speech Recognition
- Information Retrieval
- Question Answering

5.4 JOINT DETECTION

Joint Detection and Identification Feature Learning for Person Search. Human identification by names & finding a person from gallery or photos for computer vision by problem dentification.

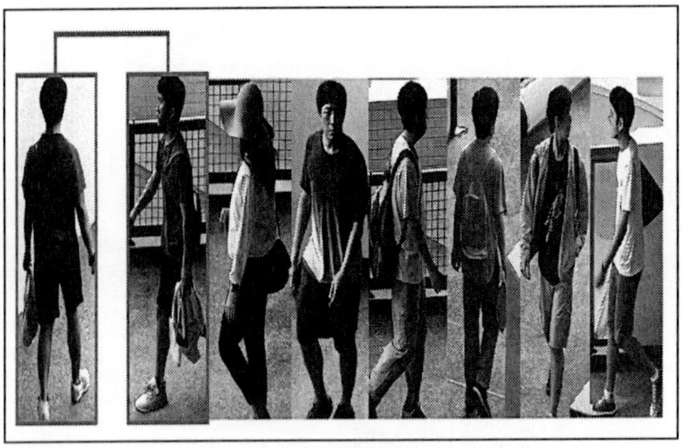

Figure 5.6a: *Person re-id: matching with manually cropped pedestrians*

Figure 5.6b: *Person search finding from whole scene images*

Convolution Approach

- **Person re-identification:** matching, manually cropped

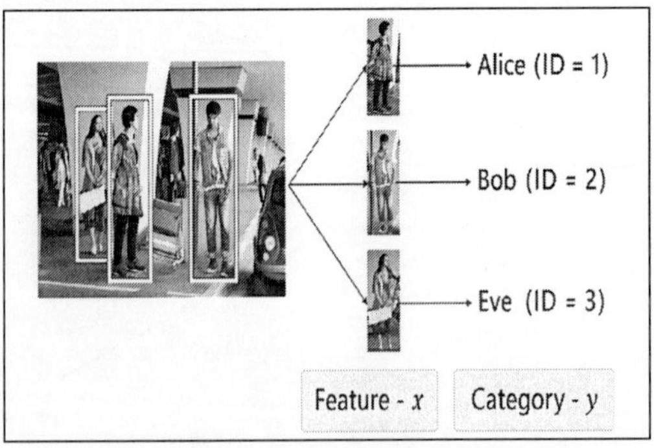

Figure 5.7a: *Person Identification in Cropped Image*

- **Person :** finding target person, whole scene image

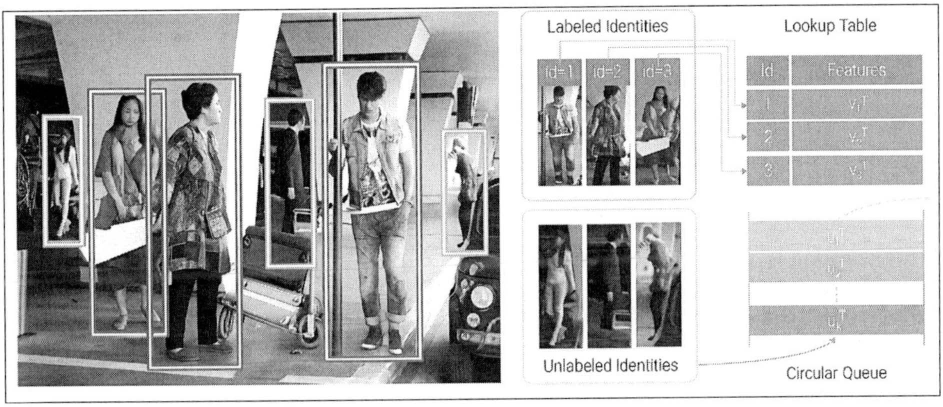

Figure 5.7b: *Person Identification in whole Image*

Steps

1. Sliding Window (Grid the Cell)
2. CNN
   - Whole Input Image
   - Pedestrian Proposal Net (produces bounding boxes of person identify & extract
   - False alarm can be reduced
   - Improve scalability

5.5 BIOINFORMATICS

Bioinformatics is an interdisciplinary approach integrating information technology with biological sciences. Bioinformatics is considered as a tool for interpretation of biological data by using information technology and computer science.

It is the combination of biology and information technology. Basically, bioinformatics is a recently developed science using information to understand biological phenomena. It broadly involves the computational tools and methods used to manage, analyze and manipulate volumes and volumes of biological data.

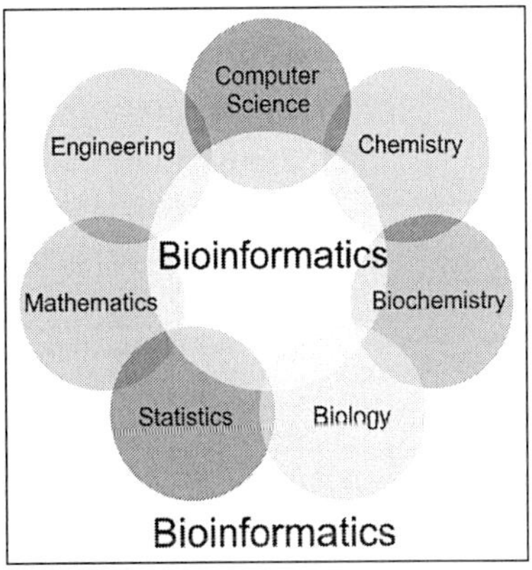

Figure 5.8: *Bioinformatics*

- Accordingly, the application of deep learning in bioinformatics and biomedical images to gain insight from data has been emphasized in both academic and medical fields..
- Bioinformatics now entails the creation and advancement of databases, algorithms, computational and statistical techniques, and theory to solve formal and practical problems arising from the management and analysis of biological data.

Bioinformatics covers many specialized and advanced areas of biology. Such areas are:

- Functional Genomics
- Structural Genomics
- Comparative Genomics
- DNA Microarrays
- Medical Informatics

5.5.1 Components of Bioinformatics

Bioinformatics Comprises Three Components

1. **Creation of databases:** This involves the organizing, storage and management the biological data sets. The databases are accessible to researchers to know the existing information and submit new entries, e.g,. protein sequence data bank for molecular structure. Databases will be of no use until analysed.
2. **Development of algorithms and statistics:** This involves the development of tools and resources to determine the relationship among the members of large data sets e.g,. comparison of protein sequence data with the already existing protein sequences.
3. **Analysis of data and interpretation:** To analyse the data and interpret the results in a biologically meaningful manner. This includes DNA, RNA and protein sequences, protein structure, gene expression profiles and biochemical pathways.

5.5.2 Biopython

- Biopython is the largest and most popular bioinformatics package for Python. It contains a number of different sub-modules for common bioinformatics tasks. It is developed by Chapman and Chang, mainly written in Python. It also contains C code to optimize the complex computation part of the software. It runs on Windows, Linux, Mac OS X, etc.
- **Biopython is a set of tools written in Python** which can be used for a variety of biological computations, simulations and analysis. You can download and install Biopython from here. Make sure that you have **Python 2.7, 3.4, 3.5, or 3.6 already installed.**
- It is a distributed collaborative effort to develop Python libraries and applications which **address the needs of current and future work in bioinformatics.**

5.5.3 Features of Biopython

Biopython is portable, clear and has easy to learn syntax. Some of the salient features are listed below:

5.6.1 Interpreted, interactive and object oriented.

5.6.2 Supports FASTA, PDB, GenBank, Blast, SCOP, PubMed/Medline, ExPASy-related formats.

5.6.3 Option to deal with sequence formats.

5.6.4 Tools to manage protein structures.

5.6.5 BioSQL – Standard set of SQL tables for storing sequences plus features and annotations.

5.6.6 Access to online services and database, including NCBI services (Blast, Entrez, PubMed) and ExPASY services (SwissProt, Prosite)

5.6 FACE RECOGNITION

A face recognition system is a technology capable of matching a human face from a digital image or a video frame against a database of faces. Such a system is typically employed to authenticate users through ID verification services, and works by pinpointing and measuring facial features from a given image.

It works by identifying and measuring facial features in an image. Facial recognition can identify human faces in images or videos, determine if the face in two images belongs to the same person, or search for a face among a large collection of existing images.

Biometric security systems use facial recognition to uniquely identify individuals during user on boarding or logins as well as strengthen user authentication activity. Mobile and personal devices also commonly use face analyzer technology for device security.

How Does Facial Recognition Work?

Many people are familiar with face recognition technology through the Face ID used to unlock iPhones (however, this is only one application of face recognition).Typically, facial recognition does not rely on a massive database of photos to determine an individual's identity — it simply identifies and recognizes one person as the sole owner of the device, while limiting access to others.

Beyond unlocking phones, facial recognition works by matching the faces of people walking past special cameras, to images of people on a watch list. The watch lists can contain pictures of anyone, including people who are not suspected of any wrongdoing, and the images can come from anywhere — even from our social media accounts.

Facial technology systems can vary, but in general, they tend to operate as follows:

Step 1: Face Detection

The camera detects and locates the image of a face, either alone or in a crowd. The image may show the person looking straight ahead or in profile.

Step 2: Face Analysis

Next, an image of the face is captured and analyzed. Most facial recognition technology relies on 2D rather than 3D images because it can more conveniently match a 2D image with public photos or those in a database. The software reads the geometry of your face. Key factors include the distance between your eyes, the depth of your eye sockets, the distance from forehead to chin, the shape of your cheekbones, and the contour of the lips, ears, and chin. The aim is to identify the facial landmarks that are key to distinguishing your face.

Step 3: Converting The Image To Data

The face capture process transforms analog information (a face) into a set of digital information (data) based on the person's facial features. Your face's analysis is essentially turned into a mathematical formula. The numerical code is called a faceprint. In the same way that thumbprints are unique, each person has their own faceprint.

Step 4: Finding a Match

Your faceprint is then compared against a database of other known faces. For example, the FBI has access to up to 650 million photos, drawn from various state databases. On Facebook, any photo tagged with a person's name becomes a part of Facebook's database, which may also be used for facial recognition. If your faceprint matches an image in a facial recognition database, then a determination is made.

Of all the biometric measurements, facial recognition is considered the most natural. Intuitively, this makes sense, since we typically recognize ourselves and others by looking at faces, rather than thumbprints and irises. It is estimated that over half of the world's population is touched by facial recognition technology regularly.

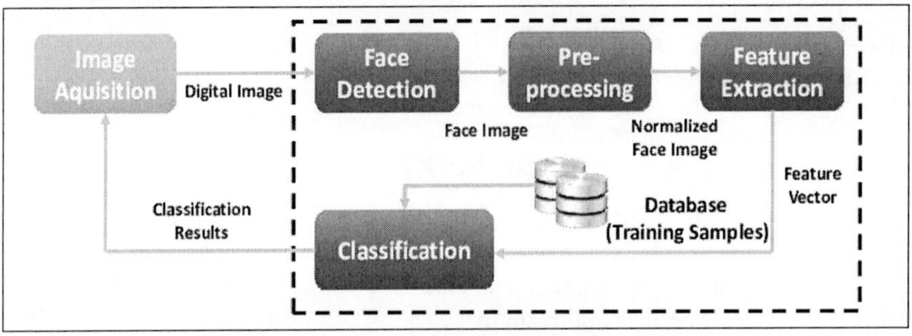

Figure 5.9: *Face Recognition Architecture*

Confidence Score in Facial Recognition

Confidence scores, also known as similarity scores, are crucial for face detection and comparison systems. They provide feedback about how similar two images are to each other. A higher confidence score indicates a higher likelihood that two images are of the same person. Thus, confidence scores use AI to predict whether a face exists in an image or matches a face in another image.

Confidence Score Threshold

Every prediction that the facial recognition system makes using AI has a corresponding score threshold level that you can change. In a typical scenario, most automated matches are made on a very high percentage, for example, above a 99% confidence score. Matches with lower confidence scores may be used to see the next closest potential matches, which are then further evaluated by a human investigator.

Advantages of Face Recognition

Aside from unlocking your smartphone, facial recognition brings other benefits:

- **Increased security:** On a governmental level, facial recognition can help to identify terrorists or other criminals. On a personal level, facial recognition can be used as a security tool for locking personal devices and for personal surveillance cameras.

- **Reduced crime:** Face recognition makes it easier to track down burglars, thieves, and trespassers. The sole knowledge of the presence of a face recognition system can serve as a deterrence, especially to petty crime.
- **Faster processing:** The process of recognizing a face takes only a second, which has benefits for the companies that use facial recognition. In an era of cyber-attacks and advanced hacking tools, companies need both secure and fast technologies. Facial recognition enables quick and efficient verification of a person's identity.
- **Integration with other technologies:** Most facial recognition solutions are compatible with most security software. In fact, it is easily integrated. This limits the amount of additional investment required to implement it.

Disadvantages of Face Recognition

While some people do not mind being filmed in public and do not object to the use of facial recognition where there is a clear benefit or rationale, the technology can inspire intense reactions from others. Some of the disadvantages or concerns include:

- **Surveillance:** Some worry that the use of facial recognition along with ubiquitous video cameras, artificial intelligence, and data analytics creates the potential for mass surveillance, which could restrict individual freedom. While facial recognition technology allows governments to track down criminals, it could also allow them to track down ordinary and innocent people at any time.
- **Scope for error:** Facial recognition data is not free from error, which could lead to people being implicated for crimes they have not committed. For example, a slight change in camera angle or a change in appearance, such as a new hairstyle, could lead to error. In 2018, Newsweek reported that Amazon's facial recognition technology had falsely identified 28 members of the US Congress as people arrested for crimes.
- **Breach of privacy:** The question of ethics and privacy is the most contentious one. Governments have been known to store several citizens' pictures without their consent. In 2020, the European Commission said it was considering a ban on facial recognition technology in public spaces for up to five years, to allow time to work out a regulatory framework to prevent privacy and ethical abuses.
- **Massive data storage:** Facial recognition software relies on machine learning technology, which requires massive data sets to "learn" to deliver accurate results. Such large data sets require robust data storage. Small and medium-sized companies may not have sufficient resources to store the required data.

5.7 SCENE UNDERSTANDING

A scene is a view of a real-world environment that contains multiple surfaces and objects, organized in a meaningful way. An image is a visual representation of something and it has been created or copied and stored in electronic form. Different formats of images are:

- JPEG (Joint Photographic Experts Group)
- GIF (Graphics Interchange Format)
- PNG (Portable Network Graphic)
- Tiff (Tag Image File Format)

Scene understanding is used to:

- Interpreting particular regions/objects to figure out what's actually happening in the image.
- Figuring out what the objects are, their spatial relationships to each other, etc.
- Ultimately making some decisions for further action.
- To equipcomputers and machines with human like vision i.e., understanding the image like humans do.

Applications of Object Detection using Deep Learning

- Image Classification
- Scene Understanding
- Self-driving vehicles
- Surveillance etc.

Classification and Object Detection

In the field of image classification and object detection, understanding the scene or images are very important to observe or localize the objects which are present. Below diagram shows the different way of scene understanding towards classification and detection. In the image classification view, if the user wants to classify whether the given scene/image contains boat and person means it will check that object alone and return the result as yes or no. In the object detection view, it will try to identify and locate that particular object as many times which is available in the given scene with the bounding box.

(a) (b)

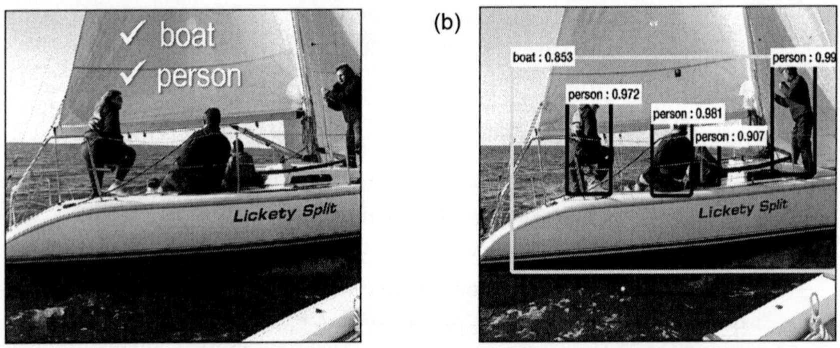

***Figure 5.10 (a)**: Image Classification (what?) **(b)**: Object Detection (what+where?)*

Challenges of Scene Understanding

- Image Quality
- Limited understanding of the scene context
- Fail to consider object intersection
- Limited object shape quality

5.8 GATHERING IMAGE CAPTIONS

Image Captioning is the process of generating textual description of an image. It uses both Natural Language Processing and Computer Vision to generate the caption

Generate Detailed Captions of an Image using Deep Learning

System Design

The entire module can be logically divided into two modules:

1. Image Based Model
2. Language Based model

In the Image Based Model the input image is converted into vectorial representations. For image based model convolutional neural networks are used in combinations and are also known as the Encoder.

In the Language Based model the vectorial representations are converted into natural language. The vectorial representations are decoded with the help of the LSTM network and this model is also known as the Decoder.

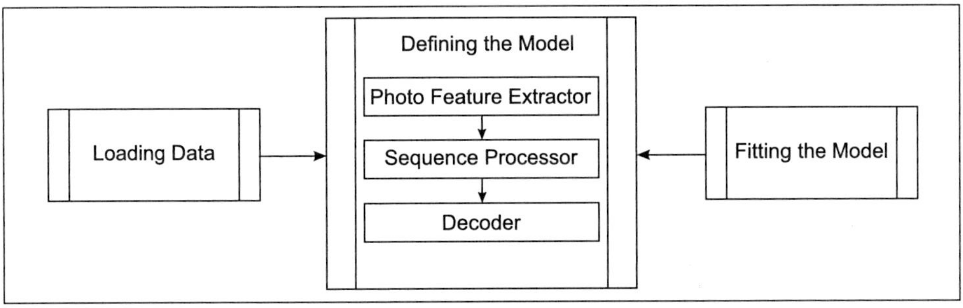

Figure 5.11: *Model Structure*

Both the models are integrated together to complete the entire process of image to text generation and later with the help of pyttsx3 or gtts we can convert the generated caption to speech, which will help the visually impaired people.

The process is divided into following logical steps:

Step 1: Firstly after preprocessing the data, the data is loaded into the model for training

Step 2: This step can be further bifurcated into three more steps:

- **Photo Feature Extractor:** In this module, it will extract the features from the image by using different combinations of convolutional neural networks.
- **Sequence Processor**: The output from the Photo Feature Extractor is then fed into the sequence processor and this uses Long Short Term Memory Network (LSTM) for managing texts.
- **Decoder:** It produces the most logically correct sequence by combining sequence processor and photo feature extractor.

Data Collection

The dataset used for training and testing model is flickr_8k dataset and is divided into 6000 images for training, 1000 images for validation and 1000 images for testing. The dataset consist of two directories:

1. **Flickr8k_dataset:** It consists of 8092 photographs in JPEG format.
2. **Flickr8k_text:** It consists of a number of files having descriptions for the image.

Convolutional Neural Network (CNN)

A Convolutional layer is also known as CNN or ConvNet and consists of three layers: convolutional layer, pooling layer and fully connected layer used for training the model.

Captioning Model

Captioning Model relies on 2 main components, CNN and RNN. Captioning is all about merging two things/images to combine its most important attribute.

CNN works with recognizing objects in images. So by merging two you will get a model that can find the patterns and images that can then generate captions related to the images.

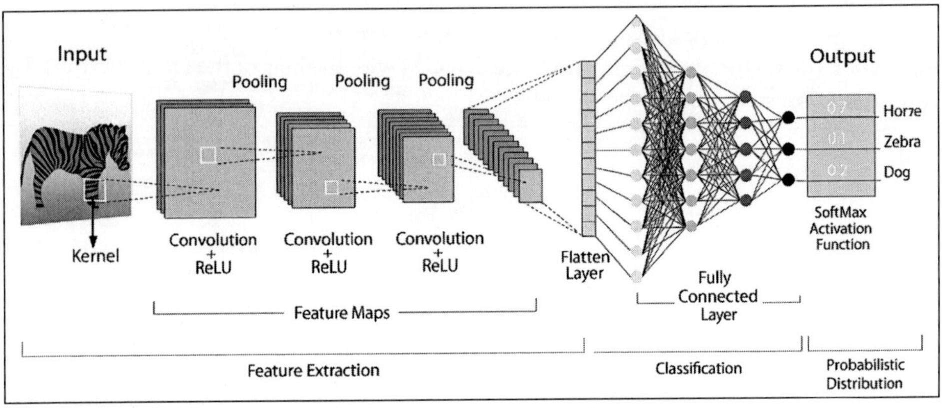

Figure 5.12: *Image Captioning using CNN*

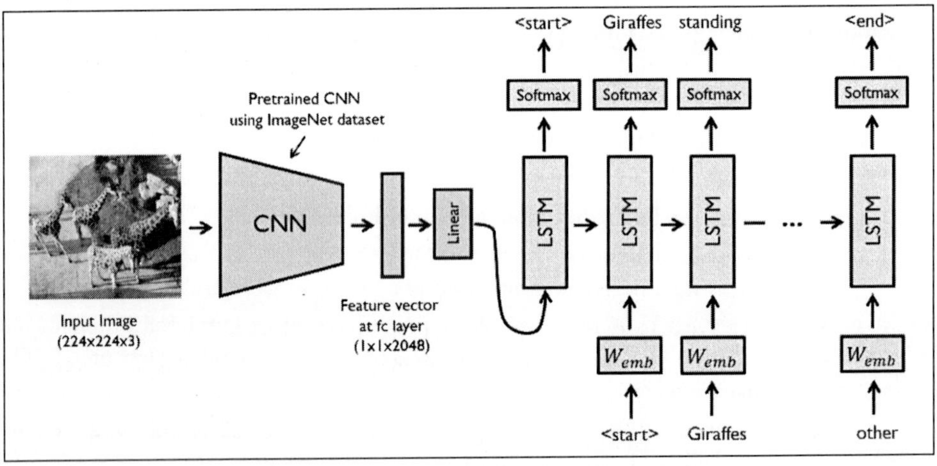

Figure 5.13: *Image Captioning using LSTM*

Applications of Image Captioning

- Images search tools
- Guidance device
- Self driving cars
- Google Image Search
- CCTV Camera